COMPREHENSIVE RESEARCH
AND STUDY GUIDE

Geoffrey Chaucer

BLOOM'S

MAJOR

POETS

EDITED AND WITH AN INTRODUCTION
BY HAROLD BLOOM

BLOOM'S MAJOR DRAMATISTS

Anton Chekhov
Henrik Ibsen
Arthur Miller
Eugene O'Neill
Shakespeare's Comedies
Shakespeare's Histories
Shakespeare's Romances
Shakespeare's Tragedies
George Bernard Shaw
Tennessee Williams

BLOOM'S MAJOR NOVELISTS

Jane Austen
The Brontës
Willa Cather
Charles Dickens
William Faulkner
F. Scott Fitzgerald
Nathaniel Hawthorne
Ernest Hemingway
Toni Morrison
John Steinbeck
Mark Twain
Alice Walker

BLOOM'S MAJOR SHORT STORY WRITERS

William Faulkner
F. Scott Fitzgerald
Ernest Hemingway
O. Henry
James Joyce
Herman Melville
Flannery O'Connor
Edgar Allan Poe
J. D. Salinger
John Steinbeck
Mark Twain
Eudora Welty

BLOOM'S MAJOR WORLD POETS

Geoffrey Chaucer
Emily Dickinson
John Donne
T. S. Eliot
Robert Frost
Langston Hughes
John Milton
Edgar Allan Poe
Shakespeare's Poems & Sonnets
Alfred, Lord Tennyson
Walt Whitman
William Wordsworth

BLOOM'S NOTES

The Adventures of Huckleberry Finn
Aeneid
The Age of Innocence
Animal Farm
The Autobiography of Malcolm X
The Awakening
Beloved
Beowulf
Billy Budd, Benito Cereno, & Bartleby the Scrivener
Brave New World
The Catcher in the Rye
Crime and Punishment
The Crucible

Death of a Salesman
A Farewell to Arms
Frankenstein
The Grapes of Wrath
Great Expectations
The Great Gatsby
Gulliver's Travels
Hamlet
Heart of Darkness & The Secret Sharer
Henry IV, Part One
I Know Why the Caged Bird Sings
Iliad
Inferno
Invisible Man
Jane Eyre
Julius Caesar

King Lear
Lord of the Flies
Macbeth
A Midsummer Night's Dream
Moby-Dick
Native Son
Nineteen Eighty-Four
Odyssey
Oedipus Plays
Of Mice and Men
The Old Man and the Sea
Othello
Paradise Lost
A Portrait of the Artist as a Young Man
The Portrait of a Lady

Pride and Prejudice
The Red Badge of Courage
Romeo and Juliet
The Scarlet Letter
Silas Marner
The Sound and the Fury
The Sun Also Rises
A Tale of Two Cities
Tess of the D'Urbervilles
Their Eyes Were Watching God
To Kill a Mockingbird
Uncle Tom's Cabin
Wuthering Heights

Geoffrey Chaucer

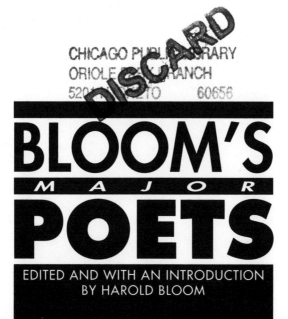

BLOOM'S
M A J O R
POETS

EDITED AND WITH AN INTRODUCTION
BY HAROLD BLOOM

© 1999 by Chelsea House Publishers, a division of Main Line Book Co.

Introduction © 1999 by Harold Bloom

Printed and bound in the United States of America.

3 5 7 9 8 6 4 2

Library of Congress Cataloging-in-Publication Data

Geoffrey Chaucer / edited and with an introduction by Harold Bloom.
cm. – (Bloom's major poets)
Includes bibliographical references and index.
ISBN 0-7910-5115-3 (hc)
1. Chaucer, Geoffrey, d. 1400. Canterbury tales.   2. Christian
pilgrims and pilgrimages in literature.   3. Tales. Medieval—History
and criticism.   4. Storytelling in literature.   I. Bloom, Harold.
II. Series.
PR1874.G45   1999
821'.1—dc21   98-49694
CIP

Chelsea House Publishers
1974 Sproul Road, Suite 400
Broomall, PA 19008-0914

Contributing Editor: Mirjana Kalezic

Contents

User's Guide

This volume is designed to present biographical, critical, and bibliographical information on the author's best-known or most important poems. Following Harold Bloom's editor's note and introduction is a detailed biography of the author, discussing major life events and important literary accomplishments. A thematic and structural analysis of each poem follows, tracing significant themes, patterns, and motifs in the work.

A selection of critical extracts, derived from previously published material from leading critics, analyzes aspects of each poem. The extracts consist of statements from the author, if available, early reviews of the work, and later evaluations up to the present. A bibliography of the author's writings (including a complete list of all books written, cowritten, edited, and translated), a list of additional books and articles on the author and the work, and an index of themes and ideas in the author's writings conclude the volume.

∼

Harold Bloom is Sterling Professor of the Humanities at Yale University and Henry W. and Albert A. Berg Professor of English at the New York University Graduate School. He is the author of over 20 books and the editor of more than 30 anthologies of literary criticism.

Professor Bloom's works include *Shelley's Mythmaking* (1959), *The Visionary Company* (1961), *Blake's Apocalypse* (1963), *Yeats* (1970), *A Map of Misreading* (1975), *Kabbalah and Criticism* (1975), and *Agon: Toward a Theory of Revisionism* (1982). *The Anxiety of Influence* (1973) sets forth Professor Bloom's provocative theory of the literary relationships between the great writers and their predecessors. His most recent books include *The American Religion* (1992), *The Western Canon* (1994), *Omens of Millennium: The Gnosis of Angels, Dreams, and Resurrection* (1996), and *Shakespeare: The Invention of the Human* (1998).

Professor Bloom earned his Ph.D. from Yale University in 1955 and has served on the Yale faculty since then. He is a 1985 MacArthur Foundation Award recipient and served as the Charles Eliot Norton Professor of Poetry at Harvard University in 1987–88. He is currently the editor of other Chelsea House series in literary criticism, including BLOOM'S NOTES, BLOOM'S MAJOR SHORT STORY WRITERS, MAJOR LITERARY CHARACTERS, MODERN CRITICAL VIEWS, MODERN CRITICAL INTERPRETATIONS, and WOMEN WRITERS OF ENGLISH AND THEIR WORKS.

Editor's Note

My Introduction, a homage to G. K. Chesterton, associates the enormous ironies that inform both Chaucer and Shakespeare.

The two dozen excerpted Critical Views are both various and copious, so that I comment here upon only a few high points.

Jill Mann offers the best scholarly account of Chaucer's pervasive irony that I know.

Talbot Donaldson, most genial and Chaucerian of Chaucer scholars, guides us to a firm sense of the personalities of the Knight, the Wife of Bath, and the Pardoner.

I am particularly influenced by Donald Howard's formulation of the "idea" of the *Canterbury Tales,* and by Helen Cooper's acute common sense in all things Chaucerian.

Introduction

HAROLD BLOOM

Except for Shakespeare, whom he profoundly influenced, Chaucer is the major literary artist in the English language. My favorite Chaucer critic still remains G. K. Chesterton, who is not represented in the Critical Views excerpted in this volume because I devote this Introduction to Chesterton upon Chaucer. Chesterton—poet, storyteller, ironist—was himself a Chaucerian pilgrim. His wonderful book on Chaucer (1932) is popular and simple, as he intended, and seems to me to embody the spirit of Chaucer. I like it that there are more than fifty references to Shakespeare in the book, because only Shakespeare (in English) deserves to set the measure for Chaucer. Chesterton, a fierce Catholic polemicist, had a tendency to baptize Chaucer's imagination but I think (*contra* Chesterton) that Shakespeare learned from Chaucer how to achieve a purely secular kind of transcendence. Chesterton liked to think of Chaucer as a continuator of Dante, but Chaucer's true original was Boccaccio. Chaucer the Pilgrim is a sly parody of Dante the Pilgrim, an irony that Chesterton did not want to see. Yet Chesterton wonderfully observed that "the Chaucerian irony is sometimes so large that it is too large to be seen."

Chaucer's mastery of psychological realism was grounded upon his ironic sense that the chivalric ideal was a lost illusion, to be affirmed only in the mode of nostalgia. Everything that existed represented a falling away from a more generous vision, though Chaucer, profoundly comic in his genius, declined to become a master of regret. Chesterton's own fictions and poems move me because he had learned from Chaucer to long for this abandoned field of romance. Acutely paradoxical as he always was, Chesterton may have missed Chaucer's irony when it is directed against precisely such longing. The late Donald Howard, a distinguished biographer of Chaucer, found the "idea" of the *Canterbury Tales* to be their representation of "a disordered Christian society in a state of obsolescence, decline, and uncertainty."

Chaucer, estranged enough to cultivate a very original kind of detachment, helped suggest to Shakespeare that beautiful disinterestedness that happily makes us forever baffled as to where the creator of Falstaff and Hamlet, Rosalind and Cleopatra, Iago and Macbeth stands in regard to his greatest creations. Shakespearean irony is not always distinguishable from the Chaucerian irony that was its original. Where precisely does Chaucer the Poet, as opposed to Chaucer the Pilgrim, abide in relation to the Pardoner and the Wife of Bath? Does the Knight speak for Chaucer when he tells us that we should always be equable, because constantly we must keep appointments that we have not made?

Chesterton thought that the ultimate difference between Chaucer and Shakespeare was that Shakespeare's tragic protagonists were "great spirits in chains." That seems marvelously true of Hamlet's greatness, and of Lear's. Yet Shakespeare, as Chesterton well knew, was also a major comic ironist, like his precursor, Chaucer. Sir John Falstaff's spirit is not enchained, whatever his final betrayal by Prince Hal, and Falstaff has much in him of the nature and vitalistic excess of the Wife of Bath. When you juxtapose Falstaff and the Wife, you find their common exuberance in her great outcry: "That I have had my world as in my tyme" and in his: "Give me life!" Chaucer's poetic sense of the Blessing became Shakespeare's: "More life." ❀

Biography of
Geoffrey Chaucer
(1340–1400)

The name Chaucer is derived from the French word Chausser, which means a maker of footwear, a shoemaker. It was, presumably, a common name, because it described a common trade.

We know very few facts about Chaucer's life. The date of his birth is uncertain, but it is largely accepted that Chaucer was born around 1340. His father, John Chaucer, was an important London vintner and a deputy to the King's butler. No information exists concerning his early education, although we know that he was fluent in French, and competent in Latin and Italian.

In 1357, he became a member of a royal household, and by 1359 he was serving as a soldier in a military campaign in France. After he was captured during the unsuccessful siege of Reims, King Edward III of England personally gave a contribution for his ransom, which indicates that Chaucer was already a person of some promise. After being released, Chaucer served as a sort of King's Messenger between France and England during peace negotiations in 1360. That was the beginning of his career as courtier, diplomat, and civil servant during the successive reigns of three English kings who trusted him and aided him: Edward III, Richard II, and Henry IV.

The period from 1361 to 1365 is obscure. He may have been in the King's service, or he may have been studying law, which could have been a step toward diplomatic service. The record of February 22, 1366, shows that the King of Navarre issued a certificate stating that Chaucer, serving as a "chief of mission," and his three companions could visit Spain. In the same year (1366), Chaucer married Philippa Roet.

The year 1367 is important, not only because the King awarded Chaucer a salary for life and he became the King's Esquire, but also because Chaucer began writing his first important poetic work, the 1300-line elegy *The Book of Duchess*. Chaucer used the dream-vision form for his poem, a very popular genre at the time that had been influenced by *The Roman de la Rose*, a French poem of courtly love.

In the 1370s, Chaucer served on diplomatic missions in Flanders, France, and Italy. Chaucer's first Italian mission was to Genoa, where he was involved in negotiations with the Genoese regarding an English port. While in Italy, he traveled to Padua to meet the most famous poet of the age, Petrach (1304–1374), who had fostered a revived interest in study of classical antiquity. Chaucer admired both Petrarch and Dante Alighieri (1265–1321), author of the *Divine Comedy*, but it was the work of Giovanni Boccacio (1313–1375), an Italian prose writer and poet, that had a profound influence upon his writing. Boccacio's writings included many stories and poems that were the first of their kind in Italian or European literature, and he is considered, along with Petrarch, among the founders of the Italian Renaissance.

It is hard to imagine that with all the responsibilities and activities in his diplomatic service Chaucer had any time for writing, but in the 1370s Chaucer started his 2000-line dream-vision poem *House of Fame,* though it was never completed. This decade brought prosperity for Chaucer: he and his wife received generous compensation from the King, for the first time they had a home of their own, and Chaucer was appointed Comptroller of the Customs and Subsidy for the Port of London. In 1377, Richard II became King of England.

Around this time, the only scandalous incident against Chaucer's name that is known to modern historians occurred. In a mysterious document, a young woman named Cecilia de Champagne released Chaucer from legal action in some charge of "raptus." (Raptus could mean either sexual assault or abduction.) Scholars have never been able to agree if this was only a personal matter or part of larger conspiracy, and the case will probably never be explained.

Chaucer's professional career prospered: he continued working at the Custom House, was appointed as Comptroller of Petty Customs for wine and other merchandise (1382), appointed a Justice of the Peace for Kent (1385), and became a member of Parliament as a Knight of the Shire for Kent (1386). It seemed that he had settled down when he left London for Kent. However, political change in 1386, when the Duke of Gloucester usurped King Richard II's authority, affected Chaucer considerably. Although he was reappointed as Justice of Peace for 1387, he did not return to Parliament. His wife, Philippa, died the same year; and a series of suits were brought against him (for debts, apparently related to investments in astrology and alchemy), so he had to sell his royal pension.

The "Merciless Parlament," in existence from February 3 to June 4, 1388, executed many members of the court party to which Chaucer belonged. A year later, 23-year-old King Richard regained control, ousted his enemies, and appointed his supporters to office. Chaucer became Clerk of the King's works, responsible for repair and maintenance of royal buildings such as the Tower of London and Westminster Palace. He earned a comfortable salary.

Although political events of the late 1380s must have kept Chaucer constantly anxious, he produced work of the highest order. He wrote *Parliament of Fowles,* a poem of 699 lines; translated the most influential book of the medieval age, *The Consolation of Philosophy* by Boethius; and composed *Troilus and Criseyde,* a poem considered by both Chaucer and by many critics to be his finest work. He also produced his fourth dream-vision poem, *The Legend of Good Women,* which was probably commissioned by Queen Ann. During the darkest period of his life, in 1387, he began his most extraordinary writing achievement, *The Canterbury Tales.*

The end of the century brought yet another political change in England. King Henry IV, who was in exile, returned to England and claimed his rights. He was crowned in September 1399, and he confirmed all Chaucer's annuities from Richard II and even added an addition. Chaucer moved into a house in the garden of Westminster Abbey, where he lived until his death in 1400. Geoffrey Chaucer was buried in the Abbey, the first poet buried in the famous Poet's Corner there. ❀

Introduction to
The Canterbury Tales

Against the darkest period of his life, Chaucer undertook his greatest literary accomplishment, *The Canterbury Tales.* He worked on this project for 14 years, from 1387 until the end of his life in 1400. According to his plan, there were to have been 120 tales, with each pilgrim telling four stories: two on the way to Canterbury and two on the way back. He did not complete the full plan for his book, however; the pilgrims never reach Canterbury, and there is no return journey from Canterbury. Some of the pilgrims do not even tell stories. Twenty-eight pilgrims are introduced in the Prologue, not counting the host and the narrator. Two out of 24 extant tales are unfinished (the Cook's and Squire's).

The Canterbury Tales begins as a group of thirty pilgrims gathers at the Tabard Inn in Southwark, near London, to embark on a pilgrimage to the shrine of St. Thomas at Canterbury. The shrine in the Canterbury Cathedral was one of the most popular sites in fourteenth-century England. Archbishop Thomas à Becket was murdered there in 1170. The blood from his wounds had been preserved and soon revealed miraculous powers for healing the sick. The journey from Southwark to Canterbury in Kent could take two days on horseback, though it usually took three days.

Chaucer sharply characterizes his pilgrims through the sketches of the narrator in the General Prologue and the vivid relationships between the characters, as well as the tales they tell. The tales are fascinating in themselves but are even more fascinating in what they tell us about the tellers. Chaucer the pilgrim, Chaucer the narrator, and Chaucer the man hovers over the narrative he created. His tone is jaunty, and he is interested in the complexity of the human condition, which he views with an irony that is, as G. K. Chesterton said, "sometimes so large that it is too large to be seen."

By using the frame of the pilgrimage, Chaucer was able to bring together and represent people from many walks of life: knight, prioress, monk, merchant, men of law, scholarly clerks, miller, reeve, pardoner, wife of Bath, and many others. In addition to this diversity, the setting of a storytelling competition allowed him to present different literary genres: romance, fabliau, saint's life, allegorical tale, beast fable, medieval sermon. Chaucer had already used the framing tale technique in his *Legend of Good Women*, and the poet John Gower applied it to his *Confessio Amantis* (1385). The most famous antecedent of the framed tales is Boccaccio's *The Decameron*, an Italian work (1351–53). Chaucer, of course, wrote in Middle English, and his works were intended to be read aloud to an audience. ❀

Overview of the General Prologue
and List of Characters

The Canterbury Tales begins with "The General Prologue," which imposes unity on the whole book. The General Prologue opens with the narrator, who states that on one April's day, he was lodging at the Tabard Inn in Southwark, readying himself to leave on a pilgrimage to Canterbury. A group of 29 various other pilgrims arrive at nightfall. The narrator talks to everyone and becomes a part of their company. Before he goes on with the story, however, he wants to tell us who those people are, what rank, and how they are dressed.

His description begins with the **Knight,** who is a very distinguished man. He loves chivalry and loyalty. He fought bravely in the King's service, and has traveled farther than most men. He fought in fifteen pitched battles, and everywhere he goes he is honored for his valor. Though distinguished, his bearing is "as modest as a maid's." He never speaks discourteously to any kind of men. He wears a tunic of thick cotton cloth, and he has just come back from his travels.

In his company is his 20-year-old son, a young **Squire** with curly hair. Hoping to win favor in his lady's eyes, the young squire has taken part in cavalry forays. He whistles or sings all day long, "as fresh as the month of May." He composes songs and sets them to music, jousts, and dances, and he can draw and write. His gown is short, with long white sleeves. Since he is passionately in love, he cannot sleep more than the nightingale.

The Knight has only one **Yeoman,** because that is how he prefers to travel on this occasion. The Yeoman knows how to look after his gear: he has a green coat and hood and carries sharp arrows with the peacock feathers in his belt, and in one hand he carries a mighty bow. His face is brown, framed with short cropped hair; on his breast is a shining silver image of St. Christopher.

A **Nun,** a Prioress whose name is Madame Eglantine, smiles in an unaffected and quiet way. She speaks French elegantly with a Stratford-at-Bow accent, for she doesn't know the French of Paris. Her passion is etiquette, the narrator tells us, and then adds that she wipes her upper lip so meticulously that no spot of grease is to be seen on her cup after she drinks from it. She is very friendly and pleasant. She is also so tenderhearted that she weeps whenever she sees a mouse caught in a trap. She wears a very elegant cloak. Her nose is well-shaped, her eyes are gray as glass, and her mouth is small but red.

There is also a remarkably good-looking **Monk,** who loves hunting and has many fine horses. When he goes out riding, everyone can hear the bells on his bridle. He doesn't care for the text that says that hunters cannot be holy men. The narrator notices that the monk's sleeves have precious fur at the ends and that he wears a curious golden pin in the shape of a love knot, which fastens his hood. His bald head shines like glass, and his favorite meal is a fat roast swan.

After the Monk, the narrator introduces a **Friar,** Huberd, as a very spirited man. No one is so adept at flirtation ("daliaunce") as he is. He is the best beggar of his order because he can get money from everybody. He is on good terms with landowners in the district where he begs and with wealthy women, because he is more qualified to hear the confessions of grave sins than the parish priests. The narrator says that people are so hardened in their hearts they cannot weep. So instead of prayers and tears, people give money to the poor friars. Chaucer's Friar is a master in ballad singing.

The **Merchant** is introduced first by his appearance. He has a forked beard and wears a many-colored dress with a beaver hat on his head. He is an expert on exchange currency and constantly talks about increasing his profits. Although the narrator agrees that he is an estimable man, he cannot recall the Merchant's name.

A **Scholar** from Oxford has been studying Logic. He is as lean as his horse, which looks like a rake. He has no employment because he prefers Aristotle's philosophical works, bound in black and red leather, at the head of his bed to fine clothes. His coat is threadbare. In conversation he is well-spoken and never speaks a word more than necessary.

Full of excellence is the **Sergeant-at-law.** He is discreet and his words are wise. He has often been a Judge of the Assize and is authorized to hear all types of cases. He receives many fees for his skill and reputation. There is no busier man anywhere, though he seems even busier than he actually is. He knows all the statutes by heart, and he can quote all the cases and their judgments since the Norman Conquest. He is simply dressed in a colored coat girded by a silk belt with narrow stripes.

The **Franklin** is his companion, who has a red complexion and a beard as white as a daisy. He is a true son of Epicures, who believed that the only real happiness lay in sensual pleasures. His house is always full of food that varies according to season. The Franklin presides over the sessions of justice, and he is a Knight of the Shire in the Parliament.

Among the rest of the company are a **Haberdasher,** a **Carpenter,** a **Weaver,** a **Dyer,** and a **Tapestry-maker,** who are clothed in the same uniform, all belonging to the rich Guild. Chaucer's description of them melts them into one.

The **Cook** is accompanying them for this occasion. The Cook knows how to roast, fry, broil, make soup, and bake pies. The narrator comments that it is a great shame that the Cook got an ulcer on his shin.

The description of the **Shipman** is similar to that of the Cook. The Shipman is from Dartmouth; he rides on a farm horse and wears a gown that reaches to his knee. He carries a dagger under his arm and he is tan. When he fights he throws his prisoners overboard and sends them home by water to wherever they came from. No one can match either his ability to calculate tides, currents, and the hazards around him, or his knowledge of harbors and changes of the moon. The name of his ship is *Maudelaine.*

The **Doctor of Medicine** is also in their company. He is well grounded in astrology, which enables him to consult the stars and choose the best hour to treat a patient. He can also diagnose every kind of disease and tell from which of four humors the imbalance in the body comes. He also studies the ancient medical authors that the narrator mentions, but he seldom reads the Bible. As far as his diet is concerned, he is moderate. He hoards his money, the narrator tells, and he is too cold in character to be generous.

The **Wife of Bath** is a weaver, and here Chaucer continues the tradition of Eve, who was also a cloth-maker. This portraits develops two qualities of the Wife of Bath: her sexuality and her independence. She has outlasted five husbands, not including "the other company in youth." Her clothes are very elegant: her stockings made of finest scarlet are drawn up above glossy shoes. She knows plenty about traveling in foreign countries; she has visited Jerusalem three times and been in Rome and Bologna. (It was proverbial in the Middle Ages that the husband who allowed his wife to travel was looking to be cuckolded.) Many voyages of the Wife of Bath emphasize her sexuality. The narrator tells us that she is deaf in one ear. She is also gap-toothed; this was supposed to be a sign of luck, but physiognomists also regarded it as a sign of a lascivious disposition. She rides comfortably upon the horse, her head being covered by a hat the size of a shield. When she is in company she laughs. The good "Wyf of Bath" is representative of fleshly love.

After her the narrator, as a deliberate contrast, introduces the poor **Parson**, who is a good, religious man, a learned man, and a scholar who truly preaches Christ's Gospel. He would rather give to the poor of his parish what the wealthy offer him. He manages to live on very little, and nothing can stop him from visiting faraway parishes. He adds his own saying to his preaching of Gospel: If gold can rust, what will iron do?

With him comes his brother, a **Ploughman**, who is a good laborer. He loves God with all his heart, in good and bad times, and he also loves his neighbor as much as himself. Chaucer gives a very sympathetic presentation of the farmer.

In contrast with the Parson and the Ploughman are five others: a **Reeve**, a **Miller**, a **Summoner**, a **Pardoner**, and a **Manciple**, who are lower-class rascals.

The first one is the **Miller**, a big-boned fellow with strong muscles who always wins wrestling matches. The narrator, in order to describe his strength, says that there is no door he cannot break down with his head. His beard is as red as that of the fox, his mouth is big, and his language is bawdy and vicious.

The second scoundrel is the **Manciple**, a steward of a society of lawyers, who is wise in his purchases, whether he pays by cash or on credit. There are 30 of his superiors who are all educated and experts in law, and there are a dozen men capable of managing the rents of any year in England that will enable him to live honorably; yet this Manciple makes fools of them all. The narrator is interested mainly in the Manciple's ability to cheat them.

The **Reeve** is an agent who manages the farms when the landlord is absent. This Reeve is a slender, choleric man, with hair cropped around the ears, and a shaved beard. His legs are thin, with no calves to be seen. He can make a good estimate of the yield of his seeds just by noting the drought and rainfall. The Reeve has managed his master's livestock since the master was 20 years old. He knows better than his master how to increase one's possessions. His thievery, however, is not caught because he knows how to make an account book look correct. He is also sly; he knows how to please his lord by lending him from his own (lord's) assets, and gets thanks for that. He wears a long blue overcoat with a rusty sword on his side. He rides last on a mare, while the Miller rides first.

Next comes the **Summoner**, whose duty it is to serve summons on alleged offenders and to make sure they show up at court on time. Not only do the summoners summon offenders, they also spy on them and report them. Chaucer's Summoner is as physically ugly as he is morally repugnant. His face is as red as a cherub's but is covered with pimples;

he is as lecherous as a sparrow. Children are afraid of his black eyebrows and scruffy beard. He loves garlic, onion, and leeks; he enjoys strong red wine, which makes him shout like a madman. When he is drunk he speaks only in Latin. But then the narrator immediately adds that the Summoner knows only a few tags, and the thing he repeats, parrot-like, is *questio quid juris* (What is the law on this point?). For a quart of wine he will allow any rascal or priest to keep his mistress for a whole year, while he himself is skilled in seducing girls.

The Summoner's companion is the **Pardoner**. Pardoners were sellers of papal indulgences. The profits were supposed to go to religious organizations, or to some pious purpose. The narrator first describes his appearance: His hair is waxy yellow and is as sleek as a hank of flax. With his hair loose and uncovered by a hood (which he carries in a bag), he thinks he is sporting the latest fashion. His voice is thin, goat-like, and there is no sign of a beard. His skin is as polished as if just shaven. As far as his profession goes, there is no pardoner that can match him from Berwick down to Ware. He carries, he claims, in his wallet a slip from Our Lady's veil, a bit of the sail that belonged to St. Peter when he tried to walk on waves and Jesus Christ caught him, and also a brass cross set in pebbles and a glass box full of pigs' bones. With the help of those relics, he makes more money in a day than the Parson obtains in two months. The narrator, though, wants to do him justice, and says that the Pardoner is a fine ecclesiastic.

The **Host**, Harry Bailly, the narrator, joins the pilgrims on their voyage. He is a strikingly good-looking man. He suggests that they draw straws to decide who is going to tell the first tale. ❀

Critical Views on the
General Prologue

ARTHUR HOFFMAN ON PILGRIMAGE AND
RITES OF SPRING

[Arthur W. Hoffman taught English Literature at Yale University during 1949–53, and at Syracuse University. He revised and enlarged Fred B. Millet's *Reading Poetry*, and contributed to a volume entitled *Chaucer: Modern Essays in Criticism*. He is the author of the book *John Dryden's Imagery*.]

Criticism of the portraits in Chaucer's General Prologue to *The Canterbury Tales* has taken various directions: some critics have praised the portraits especially for their realism, sharp individuality, adroit psychology, and vividness of felt life; others, working in the genetic direction, have pointed out actual historical persons who might have sat for the portraits; others, appealing to the light of the medieval sciences, have shown the portraits to be filled, though not burdened, with the lore of Chaucer's day, and to have sometimes typical identities like case histories. Miss Bowden, in her recent study of the Prologue, assembles the fruits of many earlier studies and gives the text an impressive resonance by sketching historical and social norms and ideals, the facts and the standards of the craft, trade, and profession, so that the form of the portraits can be tested in the light of possible conformities, mean or noble, to things as they were or to things as they ought to have been.

It is not unlikely that the critics who have explored in these various directions would be found in agreement on one commonplace, a metaphor which some of them indeed have used, the designation of the portraits in the General Prologue as a figures in a tapestry. It is less likely that all of the critics would agree as to the implications of this metaphor, but it seems to me that the commonplace deserves to be explored and some of its implications tested. The commonplace implies that the portraits which appear in the General Prologue have a designed togetherness, that the portraits exist as parts of a unity.

Such a unity, it may be argued, is partly a function of the exterior framework of a pilgrimage to Canterbury; all the portraits are portraits of pilgrims:

> At nyght was come into that hostelrye
> Wel nyne and twenty in a compaignye,
> Of sondry folk, by aventure yfalle
> In felaweshipe, and pilgrimes were they alle

But the unity of the Prologue may be also partly a matter of internal relationships among the portraits, relationships which are many and various among "sondry folk." One cannot hope to survey all of these, but the modest objective of studying some of the aesthetically important internal relationships is feasible.

If one begins with the unity that is exterior to the portraits, the unity that contains them, one faces directly the question of the nature of pilgrimage as it is defined in the dramatic poem. What sort of framework does the Prologue in fact define? Part of the answer is in the opening lines, and it is not a simple answer because the definition there ranges from the upthrust and burgeoning of life as a seasonal and universal event to a particular outpouring of people, pilgrims, gathered briefly at the Tabard Inn in Southwark, drifting, impelled, bound, called to the shrine of Thomas a Becket in Canterbury. The pilgrimage is set down in the calendar of seasons as well as in the calendar of piety; nature impels and supernature draws. "Go, go, go," says the bird; "Come," says the saint.

In the opening lines of the Prologue springtime is characterized in terms of procreation, and a pilgrimage of people to Canterbury is just one of the many manifestations of the life thereby produced. The phallicism of the opening lines presents the impregnating of a female March by a male April, and a marriage of water and earth. The marriage is repeated and varied immediately as a fructifying of "holt and heeth" by Zephirus, a marriage of air and earth. This mode of symbolism and these symbols as parts of a rite of spring have a long background of tradition; as Professor Cook once pointed out, there are eminent passages of this sort in Aeschylus and Euripides, in Lucretius, in Virgil's *Georgics,* in Columella, and in the *Pervigilium Veneris,* and Professor Robinson cites Guido delle Colonne, Boccaccio, Petrarch, and Boethius. Zephirus is the only overt mythological figure in Chaucer's passage, but, in view of the instigative role generally assigned to Aphrodite in the rite of spring, she is perhaps to be recognized here, as Professor Cook suggested, in the name of April, which was her month both by traditional association and by one of the two ancient etymologies. Out of this context of the quickening of the earth presented naturally and symbolically in the broadest terms, the Prologue comes to pilgrimage and treats pilgrimage first as an event in the calendar of nature, one aspect of the general springtime surge of human energy and longing. There are the attendant suggestions of the revival of wayfaring now that the ways are open. The horizon extends to distant shrines and faraway lands, and the attraction of the strange and faraway is included before the vision narrows and focusses upon its English specifications and the pilgrimage to the shrine at Canterbury with the vows and gratitude that send pilgrims there. One way of regarding the structure of this opening passage would emphasize the magnificent progression from the broadest inclusive generality to the firmest English specification, from the whole western tradition of the celebration of spring (including, as Cook pointed out, such non-English or very doubtfully English detail as "the droghte of March") to a local event of English society and English Christendom, from natural forces in their most general operation to a very specific and Christian manifestation of those forces. And yet one may regard the structure in another way, too; if, in the calendar of nature, the passage moves from general to particular, does it not, in the calendar of piety, move from nature to something that includes and oversees nature? Does not the passage move from an activity naturally generated and impelled to a governed activity, from force to *telos*? Does not the passage move from Aphrodite and *amor* in their secular operation to the sacred embrace of "the hooly blissful martir" and of *amor dei*?

> —Arthur Hoffman, "Chaucer's Prologue to Pilgrimage: The Two Voices." *ELH* 21 (1954). Reprinted in *The Canterbury Tales: Nine Tales and the General Prologue: Authoritative Text Sources and Background Criticism*, ed. V. A. Kolve (New York: W. W. Norton & Co., 1989): pp. 459–61.

D. S. Brewer on Chaucer's Originality in the Portraits

[D. S. Brewer, Professor of English at the University of Cambridge, lectured extensively in Europe, the United States, and Japan, and is an author mainly on the medieval period.

He is particularly well known for his writings on Chaucer, including *Chaucer, Chaucer in His Time, Chaucer and Chaucerians* (editor and contributor), *Chaucer: The Critical Heritage, Chaucer and His World,* and *Tradition and Innovation in Chaucer.*]

The quality of Chaucer's genius and originality is especially clear in the use he made of the raw material and the ideas which he shared with Gower and Boccaccio. It was natural to the Gothic spirit to attempt to gather in every kind of story, to put the serious subject by the amusing, the parody of high style not far from the high style itself, the 'pious fable' by the 'dirty story'—in a word, to sum up as much of human experience as possible, to let 'contraries meet in one'. Even in Boccaccio's *Decameron* there are plenty of serious and pious tales. Chaucer goes further than his contemporaries, however, in his variety; and especially in accounting for it by the characters of those who tell the tales. We may guess that his characters were first the product, so to speak, of the tales they were to tell. It is certain that Chaucer had some stories by him that were already written before the *Tales* as a whole were conceived. He may have wished to use these up, and to provide a series of pegs on which to hang the many more stories he wished to write. Perhaps he wrote *The General Prologue* to *The Canterbury Tales* at this stage of his idea. However that may be, the characters once conceived took on almost a life of their own, and the whole scheme continued to develop under his careful fostering and pruning. We can see a good idea succeeded by a better, for example, when he substituted the present *Wife of Bath's Tale* for the tale originally given to her which is now called *The Shipman's Tale*. The change is apparent because the present *Shipman's Tale*, although unquestionably his according to the manuscripts, is in fact written for a woman to tell. It belongs to the period of the *Tales,* and could only fit the Wife of Bath. Here is a case where the speed of development outpaced Chaucer; he had no time to complete the other half of the plan, and alter the wording of *The Shipman's Tale* to make it accord with the speaker. From similar inconsistencies in the text it is usually assumed that the prose *Tale of Melibeus* was first assigned to the Man of Law, and then later switched to its position as Chaucer's own second tale, perhaps to add its weight of contrast to the brilliant sequence of Fragment VII (B2). When this was done, the Man of Law was given his present tale of *Constance.*

The developments of the plan involving a change of attribution of the stories went hand in hand with Chaucer's writing of the links between the tales. These are no mere connections. They have been called the finest tale of all, for the characters which in the general *Prologue* are somewhat static, for all their brilliance, talk among themselves on the road between stories—and when people begin to *talk* in Chaucer we hear the very tones of living voices. The coarser characters quarrel, Miller against Reeve, Friar against Summoner. One tells a story against the other, churls tell churls' tales. Who shall say here which came first—such stories as make a pair and give rise to characters, or characters who quarrel, giving rise to stories in which they attack each other? We may as well ask which came first, the chicken or the egg. Nevertheless, in at least one case, the character came first; this is the Wife of Bath, for since she was presumably meant to tell *The Shipman's Tale*, her present tale may be thought of as particularly hers. Even so, it is not so much the product of her character as, say, one of Hamlet's soliloquies is a product of his. Her tale of Gawayn is a fairy-tale, a wonder, told in a mood of delicate fantasy (though the plot was of course invented by Chaucer). Now delicacy is not one of the Wife of Bath's characteristics. To understand and enjoy the story and its placing to the full the tale's reflections on sovereignty and marriage should be compared with the similar reflections—how differently expressed—in the Wife's own lengthy Prologue to her tale. There is a most delightful contrast between her own comic and lusty coarseness (itself a satire upon her whole argument) and the charm of her *Tale*. In the succession of *Tales* which follow hers (Fragments III, IV, V, Groups DEF) the theme of marriage relationships is raised fairly frequently, though the sequence is hardly to be regarded as a debate on marriage, as some imply. But it is convenient to retain the name of the Marriage Group for these three Fragments, and we shall miss some of the significance of the *Wife of Bath's Tale* if we do not recognize its contribution to the theme of marriage. Only a small part of its significance lies in its expression of character. [. . .]

The portraits of the *Prologue* have the same concentrated brilliance. Chaucer describes a man as if his eye were wandering over him, noticing a bright detail here and there, which he equally haphazardly records. There seems nothing more natural in the world, but this very impression of casualness, this economy, significance and variety of detail clearly tell of that supreme art which conceals art. There is no pattern of description. Sometimes the visible details of dress come first, and through them we see the character. The Knight's gipoun is still marked by the rust and oil from his armour, and his horses are good. Mere factual information, it seems; yet from these we learn that he has wasted no time after his safe return home to go on his pilgrimage. He is not concerned with a smart outward appearance, but he is not poor, nor neglectful of his essential equipment as can be seen from his horses. Sometimes Chaucer describes a person's character, and adds almost as an afterthought those details of dress which set him vividly before our eyes and reinforce what is already known of him. There is a different method for almost every pilgrim. The sketches are very brief, yet by including snatches of conversation, and by describing in many cases the opinions, usual activities, or dwelling place of a person, Chaucer conveys a strong sense of individuality, and depth of portraiture. The necessary shortness of the description leads Chaucer to lay detail close by detail, often in a non-logical order. The impression of naïvety which this compression sometimes gives may be compared with Chaucer's fondness for portraying himself in his own poetry as a foolish simple man. The sugar-coating of naïvety contrasts pleasantly with the sharpness of wit it pretends to conceal. Thus of the Cook Chaucer says:

> But greet harm was it, as it thoughte me,
> That on his shyne a mormal hadde he,
> For blankmanger, that made he with the beste.

The poetry is in the piquancy.

Not all the characters are treated ironically. There is variety of mood. All the pilgrims are presented in terms of their occupations (this is partly the secret of their astonishing variety). Then, there is an element of idealization in the actual description of the characters; almost every person, whether good or bad, is said to be the perfect example of his or her kind. The faint exaggeration sharpens the outlines of the sketches. Chaucer exaggerates both good and bad, but the distortion is more noticeable in the case of good characters, and the characters he satirizes are livelier than those he respects.

It is easy to see that like Langland he venerates the medieval ideal of the three basic orders of society, knighthood, clergy, ploughmen: ploughmen to work with their hands and gain food for all; clergy to foster and protect the souls of all; and knighthood to maintain justice and protect the lives and property of all. Chaucer does not satirize those Pilgrims who represent this ideal of society. Thus although details of the Knight's career can be paralleled in the lives of contemporaries, the total impression of his character is very different from our impression of the usual fourteenth-century representative of his Order. Even when all allowances have been made for the ease with which we detect the beams in the eyes of our forefathers, it is obvious that the Knight is an idealized portrait. That does not make him any the less pleasant and inspiring to read about, loving as he does, 'Trouble and honour, fredom (i.e. generosity of spirit) and curtesie'; he has fought for our faith against the pagan, a lion in the field, a lamb in hall. With him goes the Squire, youthful, romantic, courtly, in whom love upgroweth with his age, but who when the time of young love is passed, we may well suppose will take on the sterner duties of knighthood. Clergy is represented partly by the Clerk, who speaks for the life of learning. These three portraits are entirely convincing, for Chaucer was writing well within the range of his own experience and personal ideals. The other representative of clergy is the Parson, in whom is seen the humility and holiness, the active welldoing, praying and preaching, enjoined upon priests. The Ploughman, brother to the Parson, represents the third order of the ideal medieval society. The Parson, and especially the Ploughman, are the most idealized of all the Pilgrims, and the least vividly portrayed. They are theories rather than persons. Their poetic force comes from the beauty of the ideal itself, and Chaucer's too rarely acknowledged power of writing idealistic poetry.

—D. S. Brewer, *Chaucer* (London: Longman, 1960): pp. 107–108, 111–13.

JILL MANN ON CHARACTERIZATION AND MORAL JUDGMENT IN THE PORTRAITS

[Jill Mann, Professor of Medieval and Renaissance English at the University of Cambridge, gives a feminist reading of Chaucer in her book *Geoffrey Chaucer*.]

One reason why Chaucer is at pains to give his characters 'life' as individuals is obviously that they are to act as individuals in the drama of the *Canterbury Tales*; they talk and react to each other as individual human beings would do. The 'individual' aspect is therefore vital to the frame of the tales. The 'typical' aspect is, however, equally vital to Chaucer's purpose in the whole work. The most obvious aspect of the *Canterbury Tales*, even in its incomplete state, is its comprehensiveness. It clearly aims at universality, at taking up all the themes and styles of contemporary literature and making one glorious compendium of them. The *Prologue* in a sense constitutes a kind of sample of what is to follow by its wide range of tone and mood. The serious ideals—chivalric, religious, labouring—which operate in the portraits of Knight, Parson and Plowman, furnish a serious tone in addition to the comic and savage ones on which Chaucer can draw in the main body of his work. But as well as this, the *Prologue* makes its own contribution to the genres included in the *Canterbury Tales*, by the clear reference to estates literature in its form and content. It is especially appropriate that estates literature should perform this introductory function, since it lays claim to a universality of its own, and since its subject-matter is the whole society, the 'raw material' from which the other genres select their own areas of interest.

The *Canterbury Tales*, however, is not a compendium of literary genres in any simple sense. The method of the work is not additive, but dialectic; the tales modify and even contradict each other, exploring subjects in a way that emphasizes their different and opposed implications. Sometimes we can follow the development of one theme through various mutations; even where the unifying theme is absent, it is noteworthy that the stimulus for tale-telling is the quarrel. The overall effect of this process of exploring tensions and contradictions is to relativise our values until we reach the absolute values of the Parson, who is willing to admit of no compromise or modification—but in assigning those absolute values to a character *within* the *Tales* (and, moreover, not to the narrator) Chaucer in one sense makes these values relative too.

The same refusal to take up an absolute standpoint can be found in the *Prologue*. One important demonstration of this has emerged from a comparison with other estates material—the fact that the persons who suffer from behaviour attributed to some of the pilgrims are left out of account—what I have called 'omission of the victim'. I have already stressed the importance of not letting our awareness of these victims, an awareness for which other satiric works are responsible, lead us into supplying them in the Prologue for purposes of making a moral judgment, whether on Prioress, Merchant, Lawyer or Doctor. Chaucer deliberately omits them in order to encourage us to see the behaviour of the pilgrims from their own viewpoints, and to ignore what they necessarily ignore in following their courses of action. Of course, our blindness differs from theirs in being to some extent voluntary—for the pilgrims' viewpoint is not maintained everywhere in the *Prologue*—while their blindness is unconscious and a condition of their existence. The manipulation of viewpoint, and ignorance (wilful or unconscious), are traditionally taken as features of irony, and the omission of the victim is a functional part of the ironic tone of the *Prologue*. The tone, as we have noted, becomes more forthright and moves away from irony precisely at moments when we are made conscious of the victim, and in particular of the victim's attitude toward the pilgrim.

The omission of the victim is part of the *Prologue's* peculiar social ethic, which extends even to the pilgrims that Chaucer presents as morally admirable. The Yeoman, for example, is certainly an honest and hard-working member of his profession. Yet fault has been found even with him, on the grounds that

> no practical application of his skill is indicated . . . The description stops short at the means, the end is never indicated. The result is the impression of a peculiarly truncated consciousness.

As regards the particular portrait, this representation is surely mistaken; there is no criticism of the Yeoman as an individual. The comment may however usefully focus attention on the small part played by social ends in the *Prologue*. This has already been indicated in discussion of the individual portraits. The *effects* of the Knight's campaigning, of the Merchant's 'chevisaunce,' of the Sergeant's legal activities, even of the Doctor's medicine, are not what Chaucer has in mind when he assures us of their professional excellence. It is by ignoring these effects that he can present the expertise of his rogues on the same level as the superlative qualities of his admirable figures. His ultimate purpose is not to convey any naïve enthusiasm for people, nor comic effect, although the *Prologue* is of course rich in comedy, nor is it even a 'connoisseur's appreciation of types', although this attitude characterises the narrator's ironic pose in presenting the individual estates. The overall effect of this method is rather to sharpen our perceptions of the basis of everyday attitudes to people, of the things we take into account and of the things we willingly ignore. [...]

Undoubtedly it is true that Chaucer not only persuades us that fools and rascals can be very charming people, but is at the same time taking care to make us suspect that they are fools and rascals. If, however, we examine more closely what considerations determine what 'he would have us think' of the pilgrims, we find that they are not always moral ones. For example, if we compare the portraits of the Friar and the Summoner, we find that many of the faults we attribute to them are identical: fondness for drink; parade of pretended knowledge; sexual license and the corruption of young people; the encouragement of sinners to regard money-payments as adequate for release from sin. Yet what is our attitude toward them? I think it is true to say that our judgment of the Friar is less harsh than our disgust for the Summoner. The reasons for this, in a worldly sense, are perfectly adequate; the Friar's 'pleasantness' is continually stressed, he makes life easy for everyone, is a charming companion, has musical talent, he has a white neck and twinkling eyes and good clothes, while the Summoner revolts the senses with his red spotted face and the reek of garlic and onions. But although adequate to account for our reactions, these considerations are not in any sense moral ones.

It is sometimes said that the physical appearance of the Summoner symbolises his inner corruption; there is certainly a link between physical ugliness and spiritual ugliness in other, moralising writers. But Chaucer is as it were turning their procedure around in order to point to its origins in our irrational, instinctive reactions. The explicit moralising attitude to beauty and ugliness—that they are irrelevant beside considerations of moral worth—coexists, paradoxically, with an implicit admission of their relevance in the use of aesthetic imagery to recommend moral values. In the *Ancrene Wisse*, for example, the author associates beautiful scents, jewels and so on, with heavenly values, and stinks and ugliness with the devil; he then finds himself in the difficult position of trying to encourage an ascetic indifference to *real* bad smells. Chaucer makes this tension between moral judgment and instinctive emotional reaction into a central feature of the *Prologue* partly in order to create the ambiguity and complexity of response which persuades us that the characters are complex individuals, but at the same time to show us, in the *Prologue,* what *are* the grounds for our like or dislike of our neighbors. Moral factors have a part in our judgment, but on a level with other, less 'respectable' considerations. There is no hesitation in admitting the unquestioned moral worth of the Knight or Parson, but this will not prevent us from enjoying the company of rogues with charm, or despising those who have no mitigating graces.

I shall return in a moment to the significance of this lack of systematically expressed values, after noting some other means which produce it. The first of these again emerges in contrast to estates material, and consists of the simple but vivid similes which run through some of the portraits—head shining like glass, eyes twinkling like stars—and which plays a large part in convincing us of the attractiveness of such figures as the Monk and the Friar. The constant use of this sort of comparison creates a tone which is at once relaxed, colloquial and animated—the kind of style which, as Derek Brewer has pointed out, finds its best counterpart in the English romances, and which differs strikingly from the taut, pointed style of learned satire. Another type of simile is neutral or explanatory—'As brood as is a bokeler or a targe'—and occasional examples of this sort may be found in French or Anglo-Norman satire. But the first group, in which the stress on attractiveness runs counter to the critical effect of the satire, would destroy the intention of a moralising satirist. A writer like Langland deals in occasional vivid imagery, but its effect usually works together with the moral comment.

> And *as a leke* [leek] *hadde yleye long in the sonne*
> So loked he with lene chekes lourynge foule [foully scowling].

> And *as a letheren purs* lolled [drooped] his chekes.

Occasionally the imagery works *with* the moral comment in the *General Prologue* also; we have noted that the animal imagery in the portraits of the Miller, Pardoner and Summoner persuades us that we are dealing with crude or unpleasant personalities. In both kinds of usage, the imagery does not reflect moral comment so much as create it; and the contradictory ways in which it is used means that it is also working to destroy the *systematic* application of moral judgments.

The role of the narrator and the use of irony in the *Prologue* have received abundant comments, but they can in this connection take on a new light. It is the narrator who himself constantly identifies with the pilgrim's point of view—and that means the point of view of his estate—and encourages us to see the world from this angle. Even when the narrator distinguishes the pilgrim's view from his own, this also, paradoxically, makes us sharply aware of the series of insights into estates consciousness that we are given, and of the tension between their perspectives and our own which is implied in the 'his' of such phrases as 'his bargaynes'.

—Jill Mann, *Chaucer and Medieval Estates Satire* (Cambridge: Cambridge University Press, 1973): pp. 189–202, 290–94.

E. TALBOT DONALDSON ON CHAUCER THE PILGRIM

[E. Talbot Donaldson, Professor Emeritus of English at Indiana University at Bloomington, taught also at Yale, Columbia, and London University. Among his books are *Piers Plowman: The C-Text and Its Poet; Chaucer's Poetry: An Anthology for the Modern Reader* (2nd edition, 1975), which serves as the standard for modern Chaucer scholarship and criticism; *Speaking of Chaucer* (1983), and *The Swan at the Well: Shakespeare Reading of Chaucer* (1985).]

Artistically the device of the *persona* has many functions, so integrated with one another that to try to sort them out produces both over-simplification and distortion. The most obvious, with which this paper has been dealing—distortedly, is to present a vision of the social world imposed on one of the moral world. Despite their verisimilitude most, if not all, of the characters described in the Prologue are taken directly from stock and recur again and again in medieval literature. Langland in his own Prologue and elsewhere depicts many of them: the hunting monk, the avaricious friar, the thieving miller, the hypocritical pardoner, the unjust stewards, even, in little, the all-too-human nun. But while Langland uses the device of the *persona* with considerable skill in the conduct of his allegory, he uses it hardly at all in portraying the inhabitants of the social world: these are described directly, with the poet's own voice. It was left to Chaucer to turn the ancient stock satirical characters into real people assembled for a pilgrimage, and to have them described, with all their traditional faults upon them, by another pilgrim who records faithfully each fault without, for the most part, recognizing that it is a fault and frequently felicitating its possessor for possessing it. One result—though not the only result—is a moral realism much more significant than the literary realism which is a part of it and for which it is sometimes mistaken; this moral realism discloses a world in which humanity is prevented by its own myopia, the myopia of the describer, from seeing what the dazzlingly attractive externals of life really represent. In most of the analogues mentioned above the fallible first person receives, at the end of the book, the education he has needed: the pilgrim arrives somewhere. Chaucer never completed the *Canterbury Tales*, but in the Prologue to the Parson's Tale he seems to have been doing, rather hastily, what his contemporaries had done: when, with the sun nine-and-twenty degrees from the horizon, the twenty-nine pilgrims come to a certain—unnamed—*thropes ende*, then the pilgrimage seems no longer to have Canterbury as its destination, but rather, I suspect, the Celestial City of which the Parson speaks.

If one insists that Chaucer was not a moralist but a comic writer (a distinction without a difference), then the device of the *persona* may be taken primarily as serving comedy. It has been said earlier that the several Chaucers must have inhabited one body, and in that sense the fictional first person is no fiction at all. In an oral tradition of literature the first person probably always shared the personality of his creator: thus Dante of the *Divine Comedy* was physically Dante the Florentine; the John Gower of the *Confessio* was also Chaucer's friend John Gower; and Long Will was, I am sure, some one named William Langland, who was both long and wilful. And it is equally certain that Chaucer the pilgrim, 'a popet in an arm t'enbrace', was in every physical respect Chaucer the man, whom one can imagine reading his work to a courtly audience, as in the portrait appearing in one of the MSS of *Troilus*. One can imagine also the delight of the audience which heard the Prologue read in this way, and which was aware of the similarities and dissimilarities between Chaucer, the man before them, and Chaucer the pilgrim, both of whom they could see with simultaneous vision. The Chaucer they knew was physically, one gathers, a little ludicrous; a bourgeois but one who was known as a practical and successful man of the court; possessed perhaps of a certain diffidence of manner, reserved, deferential to the socially imposing persons with whom he was associated; a bit absent-minded, but affable and, one supposes, very good company—a good fellow; sagacious and highly perceptive. This Chaucer was telling them of another who, lacking some of his chief qualities, nevertheless possessed many of his characteristics, though in a different state of balance, and each one probably distorted just enough to become laughable without becoming unrecognizable: deference into a kind of snobbishness, affability into an over-readiness to please, practicality into Babbittry, perception into inspection, absence of mind into dimness of wit; a Chaucer acting in some respects just as Chaucer himself might have acted but unlike his creator the kind of man, withal, who could mistake a group of stock satirical types for living persons endowed with all sorts of superlative qualities. The constant interplay of these two Chaucers must have produced an exquisite and most ingratiating humor—as, to be sure, it still does. This comedy reaches its superb climax when Chaucer the pilgrim, resembling in so many ways Chaucer the poet, can answer the Host's demand for a story only with a rhyme he 'lerned longe agoon'— *Sir Thopas*, which bears the same complex relation to the kind of romance it satirizes and to Chaucer's own poetry as Chaucer the pilgrim does to the pilgrims he describes and Chaucer the poet.

Earlier in this paper I have proved myself no gentleman (though I hope a scholar) by being rude to the Prioress, and hence to the many who like her and think that Chaucer liked her too. It is now necessary to retract. Undoubtedly Chaucer the man would, like his fictional representative, have found her charming and looked on her with affection. To have got on so well in so changeable a world Chaucer must have got on well with the people in it, and it is doubtful that one may get on with people merely by pretending to like them: one's heart has to be in it. But the third entity, Chaucer the poet, operates in a realm which is above and subsumes those in which Chaucer the man and Chaucer the pilgrim have their being. In this realm prioresses may be simultaneously evaluated as marvelously amiable ladies and as prioresses. In his poem the poet arranges for the moralist to define austerely what ought to be and for his fictional representative—who, as the representative of all mankind, is no mere fiction—to go on affirming affectionately what is. The two points of view, in strict moral logic diametrically opposed, are somehow made harmonious in Chaucer's wonderfully comic attitude, that double vision that is his ironical essence. The mere critic performs his etymological functions by taking the Prioress apart and clumsily separating her good parts from her bad; but the poet's function is to build her incongruous and inharmonious parts into an inseparable whole which is infinitely greater than its parts. In this complex structure both the latent moralist and the naïve reporter have important positions, but I am not persuaded that in every case it is possible to determine which of them has the last word.

> —E. Talbot Donaldson, *Speaking of Chaucer* (New York: W.W. Norton & Co., Inc., 1970): pp. 9–11.

DONALD HOWARD ON MEMORY IN THE PROLOGUE

[Donald Howard was Professor of English at the John Hopkins University and also Stanford University. He is the author of *Writers and Pilgrims: Medieval Pilgrimage Narratives* and *Chaucer, His Life, His Works, His World*. He died in March 1987.]

Memory, central to the experience of reading *The Canterbury Tales*, is embodied in it as its central fiction and becomes the controlling principle of its form. The expressed idea of the work is that the pilgrim Chaucer, like the pilgrim Dante of the *Commedia*, reports an experience of his own which includes stories told by others. Both are returned travellers, both rely on memory. Frances Yates has even suggested that Dante relied for his structuring principles upon the artificial memory systems prevalent in the Middle Ages. This fictional premise, probably Chaucer's greatest debt to Dante, is hardly ever noted. Simple and natural as it seems to us who read novels, it was unusual for a medieval work explicitly to take the form of an imagined feat of memory: we find it in romances, but only a simple version of it. And it was unusual for a work to have as the subject of that memory an imagined experience of the author's own.

It is not surprising that this fundamental fiction of *The Canterbury Tales* has been overlooked. Chaucer the "observer" and "persona" have been fixed in people's minds since Kittredge's day, and these conceptions mitigate the element of personal experience in favor of distance, irony, and control. Chaucer used to be admired as an open-eyed observer of contemporary life (which he was) and so reckoned a naif; it seems astonishing now to find Kittredge in 1914 arguing that "a naif Collector of Customs would be a paradoxical monster." Since then, the sophisticated and ironical Chaucer, adopting for satiric purposes the persona of a naif, has been the going thing in Chaucer criticism. [...]

Memory is, moreover, central to the reading experience which *The Canterbury Tales* affords: as we come to each new tale we must call to mind from the General Prologue the description of the pilgrim telling it; if we do not, a whole level of meaning drops away. This is, everyone knows, one of the notably original elements of *The Canterbury Tales*: the tales themselves characterize the tellers and so contribute to the narrative of the pilgrimage itself. If it is true that Chaucer read the work aloud at court, his audience could not have kept the left index finger stuck in the General Prologue, as we do, at the beginning of every tale. They would have had to recall "the condicioun / Of each of hem.... And which they weren, and of what degree, / And eek in what array that they were inne." If they could not do this, their memories would have had to be refreshed from time to time, or they would have had to miss an exciting feature of the work. Sometimes the headlinks, prologues, and tales themselves remind us of the pilgrim's traits as set forth in the General Prologue, but this is not always so. True, the tales fascinate in themselves. But the unity of conception which distinguishes *The Canterbury Tales* in its fullest complexity relies on memory or the refreshing of memory: it presupposes a listener who can remember the pilgrims or a reader who can turn over the leaves.

The narrator claims to be remembering the pilgrims, and seems to be describing them as he first encountered them at the inn; that is the setting, at the moment when he launches into the description—"ere that I ferther in this tale pace." Yet as he describes them he includes details about their appearance on the road and even details about their private lives at home. Though he claims to be an objective reporter, he turns out strangely omniscient—a fact sometimes put forth as evidence against the "realism" of the General Prologue, which it is. If we ask "where we are" as we read the General Prologue, the answer must be neither on the road nor in the inn, but in the realm of mental images, of memory, of hearsay and surmise, of empathy, even of fantasy. And Chaucer draws attention to himself fictionalized as observer and recorder; we relate to him, and his participation in the pilgrimage becomes part of the fictional reality. We pass through the looking-glass of the narrator's mind into the remembered world of the pilgrimage; from it into the remembered worlds of the various pilgrims; and from these sometimes even into the remembered worlds of their characters.

This controlled lapse from one remembered world to another, this regression by successive steps into the past and the unreal, is the essential principle of form in *The Canterbury Tales*. The General Prologue which introduces it is structured upon principles of memory as memory was then experienced; and it introduces principles of form and structure which are to operate in the work as a whole. Its memory structure is comprised of several components superimposed, and these we shall see best by separating them into the features of association and order which they owe to the habit of artificial memory.

The characters are arranged in associations easiest to remember, associations of class, alliance, and dependency endemic to medieval society. First, they are arranged according to the conception of the Three Estates. There is the aristocracy (Knight and Squire, with their Yeoman); then the clergy (the Prioress and her entourage, the Monk and the Friar); all the rest, from the Merchant on, belong to the "commons," except for the Clerk and Parson whom I shall mention in a moment, and except for the Summoner and Pardoner, two classless pariahs who are put at the end. This perfectly natural order is then subdivided—Chaucer might well have had in mind Geoffrey of Vinsauf's advice, that one should arrange a thing to be remembered in small parts. He arranges the pilgrims into associations so natural that because of them the people themselves in such relationships would have fallen into groups in the inn or on the road, and we are told they did so. There is the Knight, his son, and their yeoman; the Prioress, her companion and "preestes three"; the Man of Law and the Franklin; the five Guildsmen and their cook; the Parson and his brother the Plowman; the Summoner and the Pardoner. Call to mind any of these and their companions come to mind automatically. Others are described together, though we are not told they travelled together: the Monk and Friar (two kinds of religious); the Shipman, Physician, and Wife (three "bourgeois"); the Miller, Manciple, and Reeve (three small-fry functionaries).

The well-known "idealized" portraits seem thrown into this order at random. Three of them (Knight, Parson, and Plowman) correspond to the Three Estates. The portrait of the Clerk is idealized too, and perhaps he represents a style of life (that of the universities, or of humanism) which Chaucer considered separate from the usual three. But the Clerk comes for no apparent reason between the Merchant and the Man of Law, the Parson and Plowman for no apparent reason between the Wife and Miller. I should like to offer a possible explanation for this seemingly haphazard arrangement. If we take the description of the Prioress and her followers and that of the Guildsmen and their cook as single descriptions (which they are), and if we count the description of the Host, the portraits of the General Prologue can then be seen arranged into three groups of seven, each headed by an ideal portrait:

> Knight: Squire, Yeoman, Prioress, Monk, Friar, Merchant

> Clerk: Man of Law, Franklin, Guildmen,
>   Shipman, Physician, Wife

> Parson, Plowman: Miller, Manciple, Reeve, Summoner,
>   Pardoner, Host

> —Donald Howard, *The Idea of* The Canterbury Tales (Berkeley: University of California Press, 1976): pp. 139–41, 148–51.

H. MARSHALL LEICESTER, JR., ON THE SPEAKER OF THE PROLOGUE

[H. Marshall Leicester, Jr., teaches Chaucer at the University of California at Santa Cruz. His book *The Disenchanted Self: Representing the Subject in the Canterbury Tales* responds to some controversial issues in Chaucer criticism.]

If I were going to try to characterize the speaker of the General Prologue myself, I would follow the lead of John M. Major in calling him, not naïve, but extraordinarily sophisticated. I doubt, however, that this characterization, even if accepted, would go very far toward solving the problems of the poem, because it still does not tell us much about who the speaker is, and that is what we all want to know. The notion of Chaucer the pilgrim at least offers us an *homme moyen sensuel* with whom we can feel we know where we are, but I think that it is just this sense of knowing where we are, with whom we are dealing, that the General Prologue deliberately and calculatedly denies us. For a brief suggestion of this intention—which is all I can offer here—consider these lines from the Monk's portrait, a notorious locus for the naïveté of the narrator:

> He yaf nat of that text a pulled hen,
> That seith that hunters ben nat hooly men,
> Ne that a monk, when he is recchelees,
> Is likned til a fissh that is waterlees,—
> This is to seyn, a monk out of his cloystre
> But thilke texte heeld he nat worth an oystre;
> And I seyde his opinion was good.
> What sholde he studie and make hymselven wood,
> Upon a book in cloystre alwey to poure.
> Or swynken with his handes, and laboure,
> As Austyn bit? How shal the world be served?
> Lat Austyn have his swynk to hym reserved!
> Therefore he was a prikasour aright . . .

The Monk's own bluff manner is present in these lines. I agree with most commentators that he is being half-quoted, that we hear his style, for example, in the turn of a phrase like "nat worth an oystre!" Present too are the standards of his calling, against which, if we will, he may be measured. The social and moral worlds do indeed display their tension here, but who brought these issues up? Who is responsible for the slightly suspended enjambment that turns "As Austyn bit?" into a small firecracker? For the wicked specificity with which, at the beginning of the portrait, the Monk's bridle is said to jingle "as dooth the *chapel belle*"? Who goes to such pains to explain the precise application of the proverb about the fish, "This is to seyn . . ."? Who if not the speaker? But these observations do not permit us to say that he is *only* making a moral judgment or only making fun of the Monk (the two are not quite the same, and both are going on). A sense of the positive claims made by the speaker's vitality, his "manliness," is also registered by the portrait. The speaker's amused enjoyment of the Monk's forthright humanity is too patent to let us see him as a moralist. The way his voice evokes complex possibilities of attitude is neatly caught by "And I seyde his opinion was good": that's what he said when he and the Monk had their conversation, but is he saying the same thing now in this portrait? Did he really mean it at the time? Does he now? In what sense?

The point of this exercise is not merely to show that the speaker's attitude is complex and sophisticated but also to stress how obliquely expressed it is, all in ironic juxtapositions and loaded words whose precise heft is hard to weigh. What we have, in fact, is a speaker who is not giving too much of himself away, who is not telling us, any more than he told the Monk, his whole mind in plain terms. The tensions among social, moral, and existential worlds are embodied in a single voice here, and they are embodied precisely as tensions, not as a resolution or a synthesis, for we cannot tell exactly what the speaker thinks of either the Monk or of conventional morality. What we can tell is that we are dealing with a speaker who withholds himself from us, with the traces of a presence that asserts its simultaneous absence. The speaker is present as uncomprehended, as not to be seized all at once in his totality. He *displays his difference* from his externalizations, his speaking, in the very act of externalizing himself. It is this effect, I think, that creates the feeling of "reality" in the text, the sense that there is somebody there. In literature (as in life) the reality of characters is a function of their mystery, of the extent to which we are made to feel that there is more going on in regard to them than we know or can predict. Criseyde is a well-known and well-analyzed example in Chaucer, and I suggest that the general narrator of the *Canterbury Tales* is another. His lack of definition may also explain why he can be taken for Chaucer the pilgrim. Because his identity is a function of what he leaves unspoken—because it is derived from implication, irony, innuendo, the potentialities of meaning and intention that occur in the gaps shut, by spelling out the connections. But suppressing the indeterminacy in this way involves reducing complex meanings to simpler ones. One infers "Chaucer the pilgrim" by ignoring the things the speaker "does not say" (since, after all, he does not *say* them—only suggests) and by insinuating that he "means" his statements in only the plainest, most literal sense. Such an interpretation does not fail to recognize that the complexities of meaning are there; it simply assigns them to "the poem" or to "Chaucer the poet," thus producing what I am arguing is a contradiction: the simple and naïve narrator of a complex and sophisticated narration.

—H. Marshall Leicester, Jr., "The Art of Impersonation: A General Prologue to the *Canterbury Tales.*" *PMLA* 95 (1980). Reprinted in *The Canterbury Tales: Nine Tales and the General Prologue: Authoritative Text Sources and Background Criticism,* ed. V. A. Kolve (New York: W. W. Norton & Co., 1989): pp. 514–16.

Thematic Analysis of the
Knight's Tale

The General Prologue leads directly into what is by far the longest story—the noble Knight's Tale. The plot of the tale is taken from a Giovanni Boccacio poem, *Il Teseida*. John Dryden preferred "the noble poem of Palamoun and Arcite" far above the other tales and even considered it "not much inferior to the *Ilias,* or the *Aeneis.*"

In the Knight's Tale, Duke Theseus, lord and ruler of Athens, slays Creon, the ruler of Thebes, while their armies are fighting. Among the heaped bodies after the battle, two young knights are found bleeding, side by side. Half dead, they are brought to Theseus' tent and identified, according to their coats of arms and equipment, as members of the royal house of Thebes. Theseus refuses to demand any ransom and sends them to imprisonment in Athens. One knight's name is Arcite, the other is called Palamoun.

Days and years pass. One day the captive Palamoun, from the mighty tower he and Arcite are imprisoned in, sees the young and lovely Emelye (Emily), sister of Theseus, who is walking in the garden. Touched by the lady's beauty, not knowing if she is a goddess or a woman, he cries out: "Alas that I was born." Arcite looks through the window and at the sight of the radiant Emelye he, too, is stricken, with a blow "as sudden as it is mortal." Then they quarrel about which one has more right to love her, whose affection is spiritual and whose is worldly, and which can lay down the law to a lover ("Who shal yive a lovere any lawe?").

Through connection and luck, Arcite is released from prison but is forbidden to ever step again in any of Theseus' dominions. Arcite feels that death should strike his heart because he will have to be apart from Emelye. He tells Palamoun that the dice has rolled in Palamoun's favor: "You have Emelye's presence, I her absence." He feels not only that he is exiled from all of the Theseus' provinces but from all peace of mind. On the other hand, the flame of jealousy springs up in Palamoun's breast, since there is a chance that Arcite, by using his shrewdness, could wage war on Athens and, by some stroke of luck, take Emelye as his wife. The noble Knight poses a question to the pilgrims:

Who hath the worse, Arcite or Palamoun?
That oon may seen his lady day by day,
But in prison moot he dwelle alway;
That other where him list may ride or go,
But seen his lady shal he neveremo.

Who has the worst of it, Arcite or Palamoun? The one that can see his lady every day, but is in prison, or the other, free to go where he wants, but may never see his lady again.

In Thebes, Arcite suffers not merely from lovesickness, but from the deep melancholia whose humors are centered in the forehead, where imagination governs. After two years of torment, he decides to go back to Athens; since he has changed so much (because of his sickness), he is unrecognizable, dressed as a workman. He even spends a year or two as a chamber-page to Emelye.

Meanwhile, Palamoun, after seven years in prison, going out of his mind from misery, escapes. By chance, while Palamoun is hiding, he sees the wandering Arcite, who is talking to himself about his suffering. Palamoun leaps out of the bush, ready to fight without a weapon, but Arcite suggests that they meet the next day, when he will bring armor for both of them.

"Neither love nor Power will tolerate friendship," as two friends were "beginning to learn too well," is the comment of the noble Knight.

At the fixed hour and place, they face each other, only to be caught by Theseus, who, guided by Destiny, happens to find them while hunting. He immediately imposes the death penalty on both of them, but since the Queen, Emelye, and other ladies of the party begin to weep, he takes pity and sets them free under the condition that they return within a year, with as many knights as they want, to have a tournament. He promises he will give Emelye to the one who can slay his opponent or drive him from the lists with the help of his knights.

The noble Knight then describes the temples of Venus, Goddess of Love; Mars, God of War; and Diane, Goddess of Chastity, to which three main characters of his tale, Palamoun, Arcite, and Emelye, respectively, go and ask that their wishes be fulfilled.

The climax of the story occurs when the two Thebans meet and, wounded, unhorse each other. Arcite drags Palamoun to the stake and in that way wins Emelye. The Goddess of Love, who was on Palamoun's side exclaims: "I am disgraced beyond question."

Arcite undoes his helmet and rides proudly toward Emelye. But suddenly, by an intervention of the goddess Fury, his horse stumbles; Arcite is pitched on his head and lies motionless in the arena, his chest smashed in by his saddlebow. He calls for Emelye, and tells her that he knows of no one who is more worthy of her love than Palamoun, who embodies all of the attributes that fit the lover: truth, honor, chivalry, wisdom, humility, and noble blood. If she ever wants to marry, Arcite says, she should consider Palamoun.

Arcite cannot be cured ("Where Nature will not work one can only say goodbye to physic and carry the man off to church.") His spirit leaves his house and goes—the noble Knight doesn't know where it goes, for he has never been there.

There is no end to the tears and lamentation throughout the city for the death of the Theban. People are scratching their cheeks and tearing their hair. Theseus, uncomforted, decides to build a tomb in the grove where Arcite and Palamoun first fought against each other. Palamoun is a heartbroken man with a disordered beard, in black clothes spotted with tears. Emelye, the saddest of all, also weeps more than anyone.

After a passage of some years, Theseus unites Palamoun and Emelye. ❀

Critical Views on the
Knight's Tale

CHARLES MUSCATINE ON THE CONCEPTION OF THE
KNIGHT'S PERSONALITY

[Charles Muscatine is Professor of English at the University
of California, Berkeley. He is the author of *Chaucer and the
French Tradition.*]

The story is immediately concerned with those two noble activities,
love and chivalry, but even more important is the general tenor of the
noble life, the pomp and ceremony, the dignity and power, and particularly the repose and assurance with which the exponent of nobility
invokes order. Order, which characterizes the structure of the poem, is
also the heart of its meaning. The society depicted is one in which form
is full of significance, in which life is conducted at a dignified, proces-
sional pace, and in which life's pattern is itself a reflection, or better, a
reproduction, of the order of the universe. And what gives this conception of life its perspective, its depth and seriousness, is its constant
awareness of a formidably antagonistic element—chaos, disorder—
which in life is an ever-threatening possibility, even in the moments of
supremest assuredness, and which in the poem falls across the pattern
of order, being clearly exemplified in the erratic reversals of the poem's
plot, and deeply embedded in the poem's texture.

The descriptive sections of the *Tale* support this interpretation perfectly, not only in the long passages that come immediately to mind,
but also in the short flights that interrupt the narrative more than is
warranted by what little information they add to the mere story. By
contributing to currents that run continuously through the poem—
currents that make up the main stream of the noble life—these superfi-
cially "irrelevant" descriptions achieve a secure position in the poem's
pattern, and ultimately contribute in an important way to its meaning.

The portraits of Emetrius and Lygurge, for instance, have this kind
of poetic relevance although their contribution to the surface narrative
is slight. Emetrius has "A mantelet upon his shulder hangynge, / Bret-
ful of rubyes rede as fyr sparklynge." Lygurge wears

> A wrethe of gold, arm-greet, of huge wighte,
> Upon his heed, set ful of stones brighte,
> Of fyne rubyes and of dyamauntz.

Unlike the portraits in the *General Prologue,* here the imagery is organized around no three-dimensional conception of personality; it is conventional, framed in the flat, to express the magnificence that befits nobility. I have noted that after all the description of these two kings they hardly figure in the narrative. The inference, however, is not that the portraits are a waste and an excrescence, "merely decorative," but that they perform a function that is not directly related to the action and is independent of the question of character. They contribute first to the poem's general texture, to the element of richness in the fabric of noble life. More specifically, Chaucer solves the problem of describing the rival companies by describing their leaders; not Palamon and Arcite, but their supporting kings. Their varicolored magnificence, like Theseus' banner, makes the whole field glitter up and down—black, white, yellow, red, green, and gold. Their personal attributes—the trumpet voice of Emetrius, the great brawn of Lygurge, their looks, like lion and griffin—give both a martial quality that we are to attribute to the whole company. About the chariot of Lygurge run great white, muzzled hunting dogs, big as bullocks. Emetrius' pet animals are a white eagle, lions, and leopards. The fact that these animals are tame only makes the comparison with their masters more impressive. And practically every other detail is a superlative, the quality of which contributes to martial or royal magnificence.

In some of the descriptions in the *Knight's Tale,* Chaucer is at his very best as a poet:

> The rede statue of Mars, with spere and targe,
> So shyneth in his white baner large,
> That alle the feeldes glytreren up and doun;
> And by his baner born is his penoun
> Of gold ful riche, in which ther was ybete
> The Mynotaur, which that he slough in Crete.
> Thus rit this duc, thus rit this conquerour,
> And in his hoost of chivalrie the flour . . .

Even in so short a passage, the power bestowed on this description suggests a function deeper than mere ornament. It links with a score of other passages as an expression of Theseus' preeminence in war and chivalry. For instance the very opening of the poem, with its compressed but powerful description of the conquest of the Amazons and the marriage of Ypolita, is devoted to this end, and the texture of the following incident of the mourning of the women of Thebes, which acts as a kind of prologue to the *Knight's Tale* proper, widens and per-petuates our notion of Theseus as variously the ruler, the conqueror, the judge, and, not least, the man of pity. Among many subsequent details, the magnificence of the lists and of Arcite's funeral is directly associated with Theseus' dispensations.

The establishment of this preeminence is essential to the meaning of the poem and is carried out in many aspects of it. There is an obvious correspondence between the quality of these descriptions and the posi-tion of Theseus as the central figure in the poem's pattern of characters. And like the descriptions, the speeches in the poem have a great deal of metaphoric value. If they do not operate very effectively in the interest of plot and characterization—Theseus has been likened to Polonius!—it is because they serve each other and more poetic ends; they too con-tribute to the pattern of tones and values which is the real substance of the poem. Those of Theseus again show him as representative of the highest chivalric conceptions of nobility. As the most noble human figure he presides over the events and interprets them. His final oration is a masterpiece of dignity. Theseus assembles his parliament, with Palamon and Emilye, to make an end of the mourning for Arcite. The speech is carefully and formally introduced:

> Whan they were set, and hust was al the place,
> And Theseus abiden hadde a space
> Er any word cam fram his wise brest,
> His eyen sette he there as was his lest,
> And with a sad visage he siked stille,
> And after that right thus he seyde his wille ...

The speech itself is adapted from Boethius. It is a monologue of *sen-tence* and doctrine in the medieval manner. The progress of it is log-ical and orderly.

—Charles Muscatine, *Chaucer and the French Tradition* (Berkeley: University of California Press, 1957): pp. 181–83.

EDWARD WAGENKNECHT ON CHAUCER'S UNBELIEF

[Edward Wagenknecht is a well-known literary critic and writer. Among his list of books are *The Man Charles*

Dickens: A Victorian Portrait, Mark Twain, The Man and His Work, and *The Personality of Chaucer.* He is also editor of modern essays in criticism on Chaucer.]

Two of the passages which have often been cited as evidence of Chaucer's unbelief have now been quite effectively disposed of by Professor Roger S. Loomis. The first is in "The Knight's Tale." When Arcite is killed, Chaucer writes (or the Knight says):

> His spirit chaunged hous and wente ther,
> As I cam nevere, I kan nat tellen wher.
> Therfore I stynte, I nam no divinistre;
> Of soules fynde I nat in this registre,
> Ne me ne list thilke opinions to telle
> Of hem, though that they writen wher they dwelle.
> Arcite is coold, ther Mars his soule gye!

To the modern reader this does sound a bit skeptical, and even flippant, especially with the next verse reading:

> Now wol I speken forth of Emelye.

Stylistically, this passage is not uncharacteristic of Chaucer, and when the devices he employs here work, they contribute notably to the delightful impression of colloquial ease which gives his work so much of its charm. But they do not always work, and I believe it is the passages in which they fail which are largely responsible for the reputation for "naïveté" which Chaucer once enjoyed. Professor Loomis seems to me to have made it quite clear, however, that in this case Chaucer is not expressing his personal doubts about immortality but rather referring to a question which was much under discussion at the time—What becomes of the virtuous heathen after they die? "It seems pretty clear that Chaucer preferred not to impale himself on the horns of that dilemma. In confessing his ignorance as to the house where Arcite's spirit dwelt, Chaucer was merely refusing to commit himself as to the fate of so noble a pagan as Arcite." And since he was not a theologian and could not speak for the church, he was being orthodox rather than unorthodox in taking up this position.

—Edward Wagenknecht, *The Personality of Chaucer* (Norman, Okla.: University of Oklahoma Press, 1968): pp. 124–25.

Nevill Coghill on Romantic and Chivalric Love in the Tale

[Nevill Coghill was Merton Professor of English Literature at Oxford from 1957 to 1966. He is the author of the book *The Poet Chaucer.*]

The theme of *The Knight's Tale* enacts itself through the several climaxes in its action, each of which is marked by a great debate or speech to expound it. The first climax is the lovers' first sight of Emelye, that leads to their fantastic, yet illuminating, hot-headed argument; then comes the release of Arcite from prison, followed by a Boethian soliloquy on the subject of each of the young men. Next their duel in the woods, and the magnanimous yet mocking speech and judgment of Theseus. After that—a year after—the great tournament and Arcite's dying speech in declaration of his faith and affection; and last his funeral, followed by the greatest speech of all, given by Theseus to his parliament.

The theme impregnates the poetic texture throughout and determines its pace; this is a majestic *adagio*, exactly suited to its public character. Royal marriages (of which Chaucer had had some experience) are matters of grave alliances to be discussed in the solemnity of a parliament; they are not the hasty private ruttings, catch-as-catch-can, of an Absolon or a Nicholas, that move from *allegro vivace* to *allegro con fuoco*. Yet pace, like verisimilitude, must sometimes give way to theme; the cruelties of war, the tortures of love, the pains of child-birth are shown us in what, for all its feudal splendours, Theseus calls the 'foule prison of this lyf.' The pause in the story to describe these temples is well placed, for it seems to fill in the year that is to pass while Palamon and Arcite collect their hundred knights. In each temple presently we hear another theme-revealing speech, in the prayers of the three protagonists to their chosen deities.

As for verisimilitude, the story has more than has been commonly admitted. I am not thinking of the many passages of realistic description that jump to mind, such as the harness-clatter and crowd-argument in Athens before the tournament, or the medical detail of Arcite's injuries, but of things less obvious, such as the account given of the gods, and the characters of Palamon, Arcite and Emelye. The gods are no more than embodiments of the planetary influences which everyone then believed really to exist, much as described, with 'a certain colouring of the imagination' cast upon them. As for Palamon and Arcite, seen from the respectful if sometime ironic distance from which we are shown these two young men, they are as like as two peas, and it is wholly naturalistic that they should be so, since any two young men, brought up in the same strict code, cannot but wear the moral uniform of their class, then as now, and, from their crew-cuts to their conversation and reactions, be indistinguishable from each other. Obviously if Arcite had seen Emelye first, Palamon would have quibbled in exactly the same way as his blood-brother did over the claim to priority in love. If (seen from a little closer) they have observable idiosyncrasies like Palamon's 'flotery berd', these are comparatively unimportant; for what matters is the code, not the idiosyncrasies, in such a story; if it is idiosyncrasies the reader seeks, let him

> Turne over the leef and chese another tale.

There is plenty of it to be found at closer quarters in *The Miller's Tale*. But here in *The Knight's Tale* we are being shown something more significant than the freaks of personality; the two young men are symbols for the two dominant secular ideals of medieval christendom, shaping-powers, both, of European civilisation, namely chivalry and romantic love. Arcite is chosen to represent chivalry (notwithstanding his recreance in blood-brotherhood) and it is he who fetches equal armor for Palamon (when he might have killed him out of hand) and bids Emelye to remember Palamon in his dying speech, which is an affirmation of his creed and code. Palamon bears the banner of romantic love, thinks his girl a goddess, vows himself to Venus, and continues to 'serve' Emelye after they are married, as truly as any Wife of Bath could wish.

These two ideals were slowly twinned out of the very ferocities it was their purpose to control; out of the murk and murder and lust of the men of power—the horse-owning classes of the dark ages— these codes had somehow emerged to join with Christianity in the creation of what was called *gentillesse*, and set up generosity, truth, mercy, service, constancy, good faith, and honour as goals for all to aim at. These are the things modestly embodied in the Knight himself who tells this story, and who celebrates a civilisation maintained in the teeth of moral passion, mutability and death.

Emelye embodies a like ideal, that of virginity. Part of her invocation to Diana might almost have come from the mouth of the Second Nun:

'Bihoold, goddesse of clene chastitie,
The bittre teeris that on my chekes falle.
Syn thou art mayde and kepere of us alle,
My maydenhede thou kepe and wel conserve,
And whil I lyve, a mayde I wol thee serve.'

It is not impossible that Chaucer had the parallel between Diana and the Blessed Virgin in mind, and hinted at it in these lines, and in the line

And undernethe hir feet she hadde a moone.

This iconographical idea, applied to the Virgin, appears in manuscript illumination as early as 1270 and is justified by the passage in Revelations (12:1) that speaks of 'a woman clothed with the sun and the moon under her feet': this became popular enough for it to appear in fresco on the south wall of at least one village church, in the early fifteenth century.

If these three protagonists stand for the three concepts I have named, of chivalry, love and virginity, there remains the fourth and finest, Duke Theseus. This spire of an aristocratic order stands for that Boethian philosophy that underlay so much medieval thinking, particularly Chaucer's, and asserted Eternal Providence more credibly than ever Milton did; it also asserted the corruption and decay of our mutable lives that must at last return to their source, who is the First Mover,

. . . prince and cause of alle thyng,
Convertynge al unto his propre welle
From which it is dirryved, sooth to telle. . .

More importantly perhaps, by implication, Theseus, Boethian to the end, asserts the modest dignity of human Free Will, that (under God) controls Mars and Venus in us all. It is also Theseus who knows how to draw honour out of tragedy in the death of Arcite, and such permanence as mortality can enjoy in love, by ordaining the union of Palamon and Emelye. These are the victorious themes in this palatial poem, that so pervasively is

Hanged with clooth of gold, and nat with sarge.

—Nevill Coghill, "Chaucer's Art in *The Canterbury Tales*," *Chaucer and Chaucerians*, ed. D. S. Brewer. (Tuscaloosa: University of Alabama Press, 1966): pp. 122–25.

E. TALBOT DONALDSON ON THE WORTHINESS OF PALAMON AND ARCITE

[E. Talbot Donaldson, Professor Emeritus of English at Indiana University at Bloomington, taught also at Yale, Columbia, and London University. Among his books are *Piers Plowman: The C-Text and Its Poet; Chaucer's Poetry: An Anthology for the Modern Reader* (2nd edition, 1975) which serves as the standard for modern Chaucer scholarship and criticism; *Speaking of Chaucer* (1983); and *The Swan at the Well: Shakespeare Reading of Chaucer* (1985).]

In the *Knight's Tale* the philosophic problem is why of two young men equally worthy (or unworthy) one should live to attain happiness with the woman he loves and the other should end, through the most capricious of accidents, in his grave, "allone, withouten any compaignye." The answer given by Theseus, who is the spokesman for the poem's overt philosophy, is simply that there is no reason man can hope to understand. Nevertheless, behind all apparent accidents it is necessary to believe that there lies the will of a benevolent deity who resides at the center of the great universe in which our world is but a remote point. And far removed as it is, our world is still controlled by the great chain that proceeds from the Prime Mover. Since man cannot know the Prime Mover's purposes, he must accept willingly what comes to him—and, in practical terms, "make a virtue of necessity." The poem's emphasis on necessity results in a statement that is rather less consoling than Boethius': fate seems to operate with a petty malignancy to frustrate to the last detail the wills of the characters, and its predominating part in everyday life becomes—as it is intended to be—oppressive. This oppressiveness undoubtedly reflects the increasing pessimism of the later Middle Ages. On the other hand, while the poem's picture of life is a dreary one in many ways, there is no tendency within it to urge on the reader the ascetic escape from life that frequently is associated with the stoic attitude. The characters are enjoined—as Theseus enjoins Palamon and Emily—to live life as fully and as richly as destiny will permit: if Arcite's death is seemingly senseless and unjust, it at least enables him to die with his glory untarnished—and it enables Palamon to have his desire at long last. There is a practical economy about this attitude that is both Chaucerian and also characteristic of his simultaneously pessimistic and pleasure-loving era.

And in the paradoxical attitude that Theseus sets forth, that man ought to maintain a suspicious and detached attitude toward a world in which he must be wholeheartedly involved, there is something peculiarly Chaucerian.

One naturally responds to a rivalry such as that between Palamon and Arcite by taking sides. Some critics have argued that Palamon is the worthier of the two; but others have sided with Arcite, considering him the more deserving. Chaucer probably expected the reader to take sides, but if he intended one young man to be recognized as the worthier he seems to have gone about it badly. The claims of the two are equally balanced: in any one sense Palamon may be more admirable than Arcite, but in the next Arcite will behave better than Palamon. Neither of them behaves consistently better than the other up to Arcite's death, the nobility of which should cancel any doubts about Arcite's essential worthiness, just as Palamon's sincere grief at Arcite's death should cancel any doubts about Palamon's worthiness. The truth seems to be that the young men are on an even footing and that, from the earthly point of view, justice operates with equal whimsicality in bringing Arcite to death and Palamon to happiness. This is what the overt theme of the tale, presented by Theseus, makes clear.

On the other hand, it must be remembered that justice merely seems whimsical to dwellers on earth, while the divine plan must be just; and something of this higher justice appears within the poem to lend support to Theseus' postulation of the divine plan. It is undeniably fitting that Palamon, who initially mistook Emily for Venus, who dedicates himself as Venus' knight, and who prays not for victory but for Emily, should in the end get the heroine; it is equally fitting that Arcite, who worships Mars and asks for victory, should win the tournament. But on the moral plane the issues are unresolved and remain as curiously remote as the divine plan itself. It is difficult to find in Venus and Mars satisfactory allegories of the moral characters of Palamon and Arcite, as some have tried to do. Chaucer has been at pains to show Venus' temple as little more cheerful a place than Mars'; and in the effective astrological action, lest the planetary attributes of beneficent Venus should seem to symbolize the moral superiority of her knight over the servant of the maleficent Mars, Chaucer replaces Venus by the most baleful of all the planets, Saturn, and he is the direct agent of Palamon's eventual victory. Besides, one must remember that chivalry was equally a matter of love and warfare, of Venus and Mars, and a knight whose moral conduct was all Venerean or all Martian was only half a knight. In their actions Palamon and Arcite are equally the warrior and the lover. Therefore the rightness of Venus' eventual victory cannot be extended to Palamon's character; rather, it reflects a supranormal perception of the way the universe is conducted.

—E. Talbot Donaldson, ed., *Chaucer's Poetry: An Anthology for the Modern Reader* (New York: The Ronald Press Co., 1975): pp. 902–4.

HELEN COOPER ON THE STYLE OF THE TALE

[Helen Cooper is Fellow and Tutor of English at University College, Oxford, and author of *Pastoral: Mediaeval into Renaissance* and *The Structure of the Canterbury Tales*.]

The Knight's Tale opens the Canterbury series not only by coming first but by containing within itself much of the stylistic and thematic range of the tales that follow. Its stylistic and rhetorical elevation is as high as anything in the *Tales,* but that is varied by a readiness to use simple, colloquial, sometimes even bathetic, language, that reflects its own concern with the whole range of human experience. The juxtaposition of different stylistic registers can be sharp and unsettling. 'The temple of Mars armypotente' is a formal description of place, a *topographia* seething with personifications, technical geographical and mythological references, Classical allusions, elevated vocabulary, and figures of parallel syntax, but what is actually being said is anything but ordered or ornamental:

> The sowe freten the child right in the cradel;
> The cook yscalded, for al his longe ladel.

The magnificent spectacle of the tournament and the elaborate ritual of Arcite's funeral hinge on his wounding, where none of the physiological effect is spared:

> Blak he lay as any cole or crowe.

The image is dehumanizing, without any of the nobility that characterizes many of the other animal images of the poem.

An analysis of the animal imagery illustrates the care with which Chaucer aligns style and theme. The high, middle, and low styles of medieval Latin rhetoric were defined partly in terms of attributes—the appropriate kinds of animal, tree, weapon or tool, name, and so on—and although Chaucer's interpretation of the propriety of style is wider than this, most commonly the Knight's Tale conforms with the high style. The similes of the lion and tiger for Palamon and Arcite are of this kind, as are the eagle, lions, and leopards that accompany Emetreus: these are all 'noble' beasts and measure the high chivalry of the combats, although it is their destructive and aggressive energy that is most stressed. Arcite's crow, in the line quoted above, is very different: there is nothing noble about pain. The speech of the characters is also scattered with low-style animal similes that serve to belittle their subjects. Arcite sees himself and Palamon arguing over Emily as dogs fighting for a bone in a miniature animal fable, a genre far removed from courtly romance. When Theseus castigates the folly inspired by love, he points out that Emily

> woot namoore of all this hoote fare,
> By God, than woot a cokkow or an hare!

The commonplaceness of the animals reinforces the brusque colloquial tone of the lines; but cuckoos and hares also had sexual connotations, so the choice of image underlines how far the lovers are from achieving, or even envisaging, any practical end. Of deeper metaphysical significance is the belittlement of humankind suggested by both lovers. Man should occupy a place between animals and gods; instead, the cousins see mankind as thrust down to the level of the most un-elevated animals, the sheep huddled in the fold ready for slaughter, or a drunk mouse—mice having had a habit of falling into beer-vats.

One of the most entertaining things about all this is how seldom the point of likeness between object and image relates to anything physical or visual. 'As black as coal or a crow' is exceptional; the other similes depend on some moral or abstract or metaphysical attribute (or its lack: the irrationality and moral blindness of beasts, for instance). The *effictio*, the formal description, of Emily shows the positive side of this:

> Emelye, that fairer was to sene
> Than is the lylie upon his stalke grene. . .

could conceivably indicate that she is wearing green, but the real point of the comparison is one of beauty in general, not particular appearance; and the lily brings with it other associations, of purity and virginity. She is 'fressher than the May', in a long process of association that runs throughout the passage; she and the month are mentioned alternately four times each in fifteen lines, in a way that makes the qualities of the two seem almost interchangeable. A similar effect of association is achieved later when 'Up roos the stone, and up roos Emelye'. Moreover, she sings like an angel—a simile that not only describes her song, but has the wider effect of elevating her above the common run of mortals, just as the image of the drunk mouse reduces the status of mankind. Similes can also be used to describe a state of mind, as Palamon and Arcite before their combat are compared to Thracian hunters awaiting the charge of the lion. This is also the one full epic simile of the poem, and its presence is a measure of the conscious epic element of the Tale.

There are only three lines of narrative for the combat itself: Palamon and Arcite thrust at each other with spears, and fight up to the ankles in blood. All the rest is simile. The effect, as so often in the Tale, is to shift the emphasis from action to spectacle, or to something more like pure meaning or symbol. In the descriptions of the temples, spectacle takes over the functions of both action and meaning. In the temple of Mars, violence as a principle of human life and particular acts of violence are turned into wall-paintings— though the visual impression is often illusory:

> Ther saugh I first the derke ymaginying
> Of Felonye, and al the compassying . . .

Jorge Luis Borges wrote that the line 'The smylere with the knyf under the cloke' marked the point of transition from allegory to novel. The tournament is unique in the poem in being a set piece of concentrated action, and even that is a tightly controlled rhetorical passage that shows to the full balance of syntax and vocabulary that pervades the Tale, in a miniature version of its structural balance:

> West and est
> In goon the speres full sadly in arrest;
> In gooth the sharpe spore into the syde.
> Ther seen men who kan juste and who kan ryde.

That this is the most densely alliterative passage in Chaucer's entire works is not accidental; many alliterative poems contain fine battle scenes. The lines follow only the loosest set of rules for alliterative poetry, but they do frequently alliterate across a half-line break:

> Out goon the swerdes / as the silver brighte,

or on each side of the break, or throughout the line:

> Out brest the blood / with stierne stremes rede;
> With myghty maces / the bones they tobreste.
> He thurgh the thikkeste of the throng gan threste.

Chaucer is one of the first poets in English to use alliteration specifically for local and rhetorical effect rather than as a literary medium or a set of formulae.

The balancing of syntax is often most marked when the two lovers are the subject, and again it has thematic implications. It can be done through repetition, often the syntactical parallelism known as *compar:*

> Who looketh lightly now but Palamoun?
> Who springeth up for joye but Arcite?

More often it is done through *commutatio,* where the expected pattern is rearranged:

> Of which two Arcita highte that oon,
> And that oother knight highte Palamon.

The similes used for them also tend to come in pairs, as do their speeches. Just occasionally this syntactic repetition will serve a very different purpose, as in Palamon's appeal to Theseus after they have been discovered fighting:

> But sle me first, for seinte charitee!
> But sle my felawe eek as wel as me;
> Or sle hym first.

The parallelism of phrase here is used to ironic ends, for while Chaucer sees the equivalence of the two lovers' situations, Palamon in the last line is aware primarily of having a new and brilliant idea.

This speech of Palamon's is unusual in that he is actually using it for purposes of communication. Almost all the dialogue of the Tale comes in the Ellesmere Part II; the great majority of the speeches elsewhere are soliloquies, apostrophies, or prayers to the gods. The two complaints of the lovers against Fortune that begin with 'O deere cosyn Palamon' and 'Arcite, cosyn myn' are in fact spoken to empty air. Arcite's dying speech is addressed to Emily, but includes the line, 'What is this world? What asketh men to have?', and a reply from her, either to these questions or to the speech as a whole, would be unthinkable. Similarly, Theseus' final speech, which in the *Tseida* leads into a debate with Palamon, is here absolute and unchallenged.

The effect of all this is to make episodes that one would expect to be an integral part of the action seem like comments on it. Chaucer tells the audience what is there to be seen, not what his characters see. Even Emily in the garden is seen through the narrator's eyes (he does not know whether her colour or the roses' is finer); the temples are introduced by the formulaic 'ther maystow se' of 'ther saugh I'. The whole manner of presenting the tale is equally self-conscious. A high proportion of the rhetorical figures belong to the process of narration, not to the story itself. There are abundant *sententiae:* 'May wole have no slogardie anyght', 'It is ful faire a man to bere hym evene, / For al day meeteth men at unset stevene', 'Men may the old atrenne, and noght atrede'. The proverbial nature of these is sometimes explicit: 'Sooth is seyd, go sithen many yeree, / That "feeld hath eyen and the wode hath eres" '. There are comments addressed more or less to the participants: 'Let hym be war!' There are overt devices for abbreviation, from *occupatio*—'I wolde have toold yow'—to a mere 'shortly'. Time and time again one is made aware of the techniques of narration: in the transition formulae of 'Now I wol turne to'; in the refusal to tell what is actually described at length (the great occupatio covering Arcite's funeral rites); in numerous comments addressed to the audience on the progress of the story or the narrator's inadequacy. These culminate in the question inviting the audience to debate the issue of 'who hath the worse, Arcite or Palamoun?' One is never allowed to forget that the story is a story, told by a narrator to an audience, and not a series of events. The effect is found again in most of the more serious of the Canterbury tales; only in some of the cherles tales is the action allowed the illusion of autonomy.

Rhetoric has acquired a bad name for itself, and two or three generations ago the overtness of some of the stylistic devices of the Knight's Tale was seen as a fault. In fact, every one of them has its own function in the larger scheme of the Tale; and Chaucer makes equally conscious rhetorical choices when the style points sway away from order or balance or elegance. The vigorous, jeering tone of an individualized voice marks the breaking of harmonious friendship:

> And therefore, at the kynges court, my brother,
> Ech man for hymself, ther is noon oother.

Likewise, in the erratic viciousness of the gods, the clinical processes of corruption in Arcite's body, and the flippancy with which his soul is dismissed are a necessary counterpoint to the formality and control with which much of the tale is told and an essential part of its meaning.

—Helen Cooper, *Oxford Guides to Chaucer: The Canterbury Tales*, (Oxford: Oxford University Press, 1989): pp. 87–91.

Thematic Analysis of the
Wife of Bath's Prologue

There is no other prologue in *The Canterbury Tales*, or in medieval literature as a whole, like the prologue of the Wife of Bath. As G. K. Chesterton wrote: "Wife of Bath exults in sheer egotism for pages before she gets to any story at all."

The Wife begins her prologue by saying that she has a perfect right to talk about the woes of marriage since she has experience in the matter: She has married five husbands in the church. And although Christ gave the example that one should be married only once, she admits, in all her life she never heard a definition of those numbers. People may interpret right and left, but she knows for certain that God commended people to multiply. She is also aware that God said that the husband should leave his parents for his wife, but she is not aware that He ever mentioned numbers—whether bigamy or octogamy. She doesn't understand why people talk about that as if it were a disgrace, when even Solomon had many wives. She exclaims, "I've been trained by five husbands and welcome be the sixth whenever he comes!"

When was it that God prohibited marriage or commanded virginity?—she asks. The Apostle Paul spoke of virginity, but he had no decree for it. To commend virginity means to condemn marriage. Virginity may be great perfection, as is devout married chastity, but she doesn't practice either of them. She figures these organs of generation must have been made for something; at least they have two purposes—functional and pleasurable. As a wife she uses her instrument as abundantly as her maker gave it. Her husbands may have it whenever they want. Her husband is her debtor and her slave, and she has the power over his own body.

At these words, the Pardoner leaps up and interrupts her by saying that he was seriously pondering the idea of getting married, but now alas! Having heard the Wife of Bath, he would rather not marry. The Wife of Bath responds that he should wait until she finishes telling them about the tribulations of matrimony, in which she is a lifelong expert, and then he can make up his mind. She quotes Ptolemy's words: "Those who won't be warned by others, become a warning to others." The Pardoner ends up begging her to teach poor fellows her skills.

Since she only wants to amuse, she asks that nobody in the company take offense at her words, and she then relates stories regarding her many husbands.

Three of them were good, and two bad. It happened that those who were good were also rich and old. The Wife of Bath ruled them so well that they were perfectly happy. After that she talks about what is the best way to talk to a husband in order to have him under one's control. Her method is to accuse them of being at fault. When the men say that woman's chastity is in danger if they put on nice clothes and wear splendid jewelry—she takes as much notice of his saying as a flea. If Mr. Brute thinks that she is looking smart because she wants to run out and parade her miserable rags—he is wrong. And if Sir Old Fool thinks that there is any use in spying on her— he is again wrong. If he begs Argus with his hundred eyes to guard her, he wouldn't be able to keep watch unless she wants him to. She always strikes first with her reproaches, and in that way, stops their strife.

She would accuse her husband of wenching when he was so sick he could hardly stand; yet he liked it, because he thought it showed how much she loved him. When she walked around at night, she covered herself by saying it was to spy on the girls he slept with. In bed, as soon as she felt her husband's arm over her, she wouldn't stay one minute until he would ransom himself to her. And then she would let him "do his foolishness." The Wife of Bath cheerfully comments: "As always everything has its price." In order to get what she wants she will put up with his lust and pretend that is what she wants, though she has never liked "old bacon." In their arguments, she would tell him that since a man is more rational than a woman, he had to be the one to give way.

This is how it was with her three husbands. After this she turns to tell us about her fourth.

"My fourth husband was a rake, that is to say he kept a mistress." (My ferthe housbonde was a revelour—/That is to sayn, he hadde a paramour—). She made him suffer for that. She pretended she was interested in other men and to make him cook in his own grease with jealousy. She is proud to say that she was his Purgatory on Earth.

Her fifth husband, Jankin, whom she took for love not for money, was an Oxford scholar. She was twice his age. She seduced him while she was still with her fourth husband. She made a mistake which she bitterly regretted afterward: She gave him all the lands and rents that had been given to her. He would beat every bone of her body and yet would be able to win her love in a moment. She admits that she loved him best because he was free of his love to her. Women have a strange fancy in these matters: Whatever is not easily to be had, they'll beg for it. On the other hand, pursue them, and they will run away. Jankin would read all the books about the unfaithful wicked women in history and lecture her about it. He would quote proverbs from Ecclesiastics, Valeirus, Theophrastus, Tertulian, Parables of Solomon, but all in vain—she wouldn't yield. She would not bear a man who criticizes her. And anyway, it is impossible for any scholar to speak well of women, except of the lives of female saints.

The Wife of Bath comes to the conclusion of her Prologue by telling the pilgrims how she succeeded in taking control of her fifth husband. One evening, he sat her down and made her listen to his favorite stories of women's atrocious behavior, from Samson's wife to Dejenira, Hercules' wife, Socrates' two wives, then Clytemnestra, Livia, and Lucia, and when she realized he would never finish reading the accursed book, she tore up three pages from it and punched him with her fist on his cheek, so that he tumbled backward. He jumped up and gave her a punch in the head, and she fell on the floor. She pretended she was dying and begged him to promise he would never hit her again. Before she supposedly was about to die, she struck him once again. But he had already promised her, and they made up. He finally gave over the reins of their marriage to her.

The tale that follows further considers the question of supremacy. ❀

Thematic Analysis of the
Wife of Bath's Tale

The Wife of Bath's Tale was written specifically for her. It belongs to the genre of romance and folktale and sets the theme of sovereignty and the nature of marriage.

In King Arthur's court was a young knight, who, one day while he was riding through the countryside, happened to spot a maiden walking by herself. He took her maidenhood by force, and for this King Arthur condemned him to death. The Queen and other ladies begged the King for mercy, until he, at last, granted him life. The knight was handed over to the Queen so that she might decide what to do with him. She told him that his life was not safe yet, and it never would be, if he didn't tell her what it was that women most desire. The knight couldn't give her an answer right away, and she gave him a year to find the answer.

He set off and visited every place where he thought he could find the answer. Some women said they loved wealth the most; some said honor; some said wantonness; some rich attire; some loved the pleasures of the bed. Some claimed that women's hearts were most satisfied when they were flattered, with which the Wife of Bath agrees. "A man can win woman best by flattery" (A man shal winne us best with flaterye). Some said women loved best their freedom to do what pleases them. Others said women take most delight in being thought to be dependable, not capable of betrayal. In order to show how women cannot keep anything secret the Wife of Bath digresses by telling the story of Midas, who had asses' ears under his hair and whose wife did keep it a secret.

The knight couldn't find his answer and time was running out. On his way back home, he met an old woman and hopelessly asked her to help him. She demanded that he pledge his word that he would do the first thing she asked him. He promised her, and she whispered her directive in his ear.

Before the Queen and many matrons, maids, and widows assembled he said he learned the answer.

"My lige lady, generally," quod he,
"Wommen desire to have sovereinetee
As wel oveer hir housbonde as hir love,
And for to been in maistrye him above."

No one contradicted; all declared he was right and he earned his life. The old woman told the Court that she had taught the knight the answer and that in exchange she asked him to marry her. Despite her ugliness and old age, the knight couldn't do anything but take her as wife.

On their wedding night, the knight suffered anguish of mind. He tossed and turned in bed and the old woman smiled. She asked him if every knight behaved like this with his wife. He admitted that although she had saved his life, she was physically so unappealing that it shouldn't surprise her that he tossed and turned. A long discourse on the virtue of *gentillesse* follows. Chaucer's conclusion is that true nobility comes by grace; if someone does not perform noble deeds, all his noble ancestry, be it duke's or earl's, is in vain.

Faced by the choice given by his wife either to have an old but faithful hag or a young and fair woman who attracts other men as well, the knight, after thinking it over, lets his wife choose. She asked him if she had gained mastery over him, and when he said yes, she told him that she would be a beautiful as well as a true wife to him. When she turned into a young and lovely woman, he kissed her a thousand times in a row, and they lived in perfect happiness ever after. ❀

Critical Views on the
Wife of Bath's Prologue and Tale

CHARLES MUSCATINE ON THE WIFE OF BATH'S "LEARNINGS"

[Charles Muscatine is Professor of English at the University of California, Berkeley. He is the author of *Chaucer and the French Tradition.*]

But though the Wife is possibly the most fully realized character in Chaucer, her characterization accounts for only one part of the *Prologue.* The poem derives as much weight from the wealth of doctrine, *sentence,* and *exemplum* it incorporates. This material is amassed to represent the points of view opposed to the Wife, and only with its assistance does Chaucer achieve depth, and the compendiousness that Justinus recommends. The actual extent of the Wife's "learning," once a scholarly eye pieces it together, is quite astounding:

> In the eight hundred twenty-eight lines of her *Prologue* she refers . . . to Jesus, Solomon, St. Paul, Lamech, Abraham, Jacob, Mark, Ptolemy, Argus, Job, Metellius, Venus, Darius, Appelles, Mars, Simplicius Gallus, Ecclesiastes, Valerius, Theophrastus, Jerome, Jovinian, Tertullian, Chrysippus, Trotula, Héloïse, Ovid, Midas, Adam, Mercury, Eve, Sampson, Hercules, Dejanira, Socrates, Xantippe, Pasiphaë, Clytemnestra, Amphiaraus, Eriphyle, Livia, Lucilia, Latumyus, (whoever he is), and Arrius, not to mention the various saints by whom she swears—an average of better than one new literary or mythological reference to every twenty lines.

The assimilation of this mass of material is one of the stylistic triumphs of the *Prologue.* It shows how deeply Chaucer feels the "meaning" of his form, how closely he respects the artistic assumptions behind it. Whereas Jean de Meun had unblushingly put undigested learning into the mouth of his character at every turn, regardless of the detriment to the characterization, Chaucer does everything he can to smuggle it in under a realistic disguise. But his will to keep the realism of characterization inviolate has nothing to do with a general striving for verisimilitude. What wife was ever so learned or pedantic as Prudence in Chaucer's *Melibee?* How can one defend as verisimilitude Dorigen's learned complaint in the *Franklin's Tale?* The careful naturalization of the Wife's authorities (as opposed to the frank conventionalism of the other cases) arises from the fact that the naturalistic style is essential to the symbolism of the Wife's attitudes, but not to Prudence's prudence nor to Dorigen's *sorwe* and *trouthe*. Though the Prologue may have been intended to follow the Nun's Priest's Tale, and thus to stand in some relationship to the matrimonial matter therein, as we have it there is no link with what goes before. It begins in a vacuum. That this has been little disadvantage (Kittredge thought it began his "Marriage Group" of tales) is testimony to Chaucer' success in developing the controversy from within. The doctrinal authorities extend vastly the sphere of the *Prologue*'s meaning and provide the issues that feed its argument. But they do not usurp the Wife's voice; their inherent disagreement with the Wife's nature is never allowed to weaken the poetry of her own position. Chaucer solved here a problem comparable to Jean de Meun's problem with Faus-Semblant. Jean's patience, or his grasp of the technique of naturalism, was not equal to the delicate operation required. Chaucer's was.

The most obvious means of giving the doctrinal material a naturalistic cast is seen in Chaucer's choice of examples. He drew on a variety of traditional authorities, notably Jean de Meun, the *Miroir de mariage* of Deschamps, the epistle of Jerome against Jovinian with its fragment of Theophrastus' *Liber Aureolus de Nuptiis*, and Walter Map's *Epistola Valerii ad Rufinum*. Anti-feminist doctrine is presented in these works in a variety of forms. Chaucer chooses much from what is already cast in familiar, realistic terms. [. . .]

Many of Chaucer's borrowings, and adaptations [. . .] are of course only appreciable by scholars, by reference to the textual sources. The fact of such borrowing and adaptation, while it tells us something about Chaucer's method, is not a part of the public meaning of the poem, and is not detectible by ordinary stylistic analysis. But there is another powerful class of naturalizing devices in the surface rhetoric. Even where the doctrinal material is nakedly learned or conventional, it appears in the *Prologue* in an altered guise. The issue in the opening section turns on Biblical authority for remarriage. Chaucer does not go to the trouble of establishing the fact that the Wife is a Biblical scholar before having her cite John iv, 17–18. Rather, he eliminates the problem of verisimilitude stylistically. In the oral recitation of passages like the following, naked texualism is swallowed up by the dramatics of the delivery:

"But me was toold, nat longe agoon is,
That sith that Crist ne wente nevere but onis
To weddyng, in the Cane of Galilee,
That by the same ensample taughte he me
That I ne sholde wedded be but ones.
Herkne eek, lo, which a sharp word for the nones,
Biside a welle, Jhesus, God and man,
Spak in repreeve of the Samaritan;
'Thou has yhad fyve housboundes,' quod he,
'And that ilke man that now hath thee
Is nought thyn housbounde,' *thus seyde he certeyn.*
What that he mente thereby, I can nat seyn;
But that I axe, why that the fifthe man
Was noon housbounde to the Samaritan?
How many might she have in mariage?
Yet herde I nevere tellen in myn age
Upon this nombre diffinicioun.

Besides the obvious device of attributing the learning to hearsay, phrases such as "Herkne eek," typical of dramatic monologue, continually refresh the illusion of an actual speaker and an actual audience. The personal comment and evaluation, and the repeated, combative querying, as "How manye myghte she have in mariage?" give the textual material a dynamic quality that we do not find in the conventional idiom. They move both speaker and audience to take issue, as the doctrinal passages in the *Knight's Tale,* for instance, do not. And unlike the passages in the *Knight's Tale,* these have a broken, turbulent rhythm which reduces their structural isolation and sweeps them into the current of the Wife of Bath's naturalistic character.

—Charles Muscatine, *Chaucer and the French Tradition* (Berkeley: University of California Press, 1957): pp. 206–10.

EDWARD WAGENKNECHT ON THE WIFE OF
BATH'S SENSUALITY

[Edward Wagneknecht is a well-known literary critic and writer. Among his list of books are *The Man Charles Dickens: A Victorian Portrait, Mark Twain: The Man and His*

Work, and *The Personality of Chaucer.* He is also editor of
modern essays in criticism on Chaucer.]

Like all who have lived sensual lives primarily, the Wife finds
growing old a tragedy. As Manly has told us, her headdress is a generation out of date, and for her who boasted that she was never
without "purveiaunce" in marriage, the lusty succession at last has
failed. Husband #5 is dead, but Husband #6 is not knocking at the
door, and probably will not knock. It may even be that she has gone
on the pilgrimage to find him, and that her audacious Prologue is a
frank setting-forth of her wares.

> "But, Lord Crist! whan that it remembreth me
> Upon my yowthe, and on my jolitee,
> It tikleth me aboute myn herte roote.
> Unto this day it dooth myn herte boote
> That I have had my world as in my tyme."

This is one of the great dramatic utterances of literature, but surely it
is also very sad. "Remembreth," "have had," "as in my tyme"—these
are the key words. The good time is past, and it will never come
again.

Yet she is not quite like Falstaff or Mrs. Gamp, for she is much
more respectable than either. She is a working woman and an
artisan—

> Of clooth-mayking she hadde swich an haunt,
> She passed hem of Ypres and of Gaunt—

and she maintained her standing in the community as neither of the
others did:

> She was a worthy womman al hir lyve.

Falstaff, to be sure, is a knight, and Mrs. Gamp is a nurse. But Falstaff goes to war not to fight but to play possum and flourish a bottle
instead of a pistol, and Mrs. Gamp goes nursing to put her mouth to
the bottle "on the chimley piece" and to steal her patient's pillow
because her easy chair is "harder than a brick-badge."

We cannot even be sure that the Wife has committed adultery,
though she has certainly fornicated:

> Housbondes at chirche dore she hadde fyve,
> Withouten oother compaignye in youthe.

The "compaignye" was carnal, surely, but this was before she was married. In certain passages she seems to suggest that she claimed extramarital freedom for herself, and she certainly flirted with Jankyn while his predecessor was still alive, but there is at least one passage in which she specifically denies adultery:

> "Now wol I tellen of my fourthe housbonde.
> I seye, I hadde in herte greet despit
> That he of any other had delit.
> But he had quit, by God and by Seint Joce!
> I mad hym of the same wode a croce;
> Nat of my body, in no foul manere,
> But certeinly, I made folk swich cheere
> That in his ownene grece I made hym frye
> For angre, and for verray jalousye."

It may be, as John Speirs suggests, that the Wife's temperamental affinity is with the nature-cults or "fayerye" which she refers to so boldly and so charmingly at the beginning of her tale, but if so it is only her desires which are pagan; her mind has never questioned the fundamental Christian values.

> "Allas! allas! that evere love was synne!"

It is a cry which, as Lowes has remarked, "sums up half the passion and pain of the world," and nobody has said more. But it has meaning only for those who inherit the Jewish-Christian ethic. For pagans love was never "synne." As the Reverend Mr. Davidson's wife points out in Colton and Randolph's *Rain*, when she and her husband went to the South Sea as missionaries, they had to "teach" the natives "what sin is."

The Wife hates virginity, yet she accepts the basic medieval notion that it is nobler than sexuality. She has read and pondered with some intelligence and discrimination what the Bible has to say about sex and marriage, and she has no doubts concerning any of the basic Christian doctrines. Her fundamental, unanswerable objection to virginity—that if all women were content to remain virgins, there could be no more virgins—echoes St. Jerome, and she is quite in harmony with St. Thomas Aquinas and Catholic teaching in general that continence is not required of all. She distinguishes sharply between what is commanded of Christians and what is only suggested as a counsel of perfection, and she ignores the latter because, as she says frankly, perfection does not appeal to her, but she neither denies its possibility for others nor despises it in them. There is even an attractive element of Christian humility in her attitude toward herself on this point. You may have gold dishes in your house, she says, but you do not use these every day, for you have wooden dishes too, and these have their use and value. In another passage, she herself is hot barley bread, set over against the pure wheat of the virgins. It should be noted, also, that she has a horror of perverted sexuality which matches that expressed, for whatever reason, by the Man of Law in his Introduction, and this, I would venture to guess, Chaucer himself shared.

—Edward Wagenknecht, *The Personality of Chaucer* (Norman, Okla.: University of Oklahoma Press, 1968): pp. 95–98.

D. S. BREWER ON THE WIFE OF BATH'S COMMENTARY ON WOMEN

[D. S. Brewer, Professor of English at the University of Cambridge, has lectured extensively in Europe, the United States, and Japan on the medieval period. He is particularly well known for his writings on Chaucer, including *Chaucer, Chaucer in His Time, Chaucer and Chaucerians* (editor and contributor), *Chaucer: The Critical Heritage, Chaucer and His World,* and *Tradition and Innovation in Chaucer.*]

And indeed the Wife of Bath's theme (for it his her cheerful, arrogant voice we hear) is tribulation in marriage—particularly the misery she has caused her five successive husbands. Chaucer draws on the antifeminist literature of an antifeminist age as material for his supreme feminist to use in her assertion of female rights, and her very assertion is a superb satire on women. Imagine being married to the Wife of Bath! Flesh and spirit quail before her insatiable appetite, her incessant talk, her joyously predatory vitality. We laugh at her only because, seeing the danger, we know we are safe. While she was alive the joke was on her husbands: for the rest of the time it is on her, the supreme justification of all the bad things 'thise olde wyse' have ever said about women. Her Prologue, a glorious comedy of wifely oppression, is in a way similar to the Pardoner's in that it is a confession, revealing all the immodest tricks of her successful domination, all her womanly vices. The relation of her tale to her Prologue is also a little similar, since it contradicts her professed conviction. Once the husband in her story had granted his wife what women want most in all the world—sovereignty—then

> she obeyed hym in every thyng
> That myghte doon hym plesance or likyng.

But the Wife goes on to ask—as the Pardoner had asked for alms—for

> Housbondes meeke, yonge, and fressh abedde,
> And grace t'overbyde hem that we wedde;

—a request which no more arises out of her tale than the Pardoner's request did from his. The implication of the Wife's tale is that the husband and wife should each yield the other the 'mastery'. She is condemned out of her own mouth.

But from our safe distance we love her, as we love the cowardly cheat Falstaff. Her enjoyment of life and of her own successes communicates itself to us. High spirits and laughter are infectious. Far from detecting in her, as do some critics, any underlying insecurity, any near-tragic need for love, we see in her only the energy, luxuriousness, joyfulness, cunning, of the daughter of Mars and Venus. She gladly grants virginity its superior place, but

> everich hath of God a propre yifte,

and she will envy no virginity in the full and joyful practice of her own gift

> God bad us for to wexe and multiply;
> That gentil texte kan I wel understonde.

However, she does not love marriage for the joys of the family circle.

Her tale centers on the twofold problem of what women most desire, and what should be the proper marriage relationship. The religious and legal doctrine of the husband's headship of the wife is set against the love-doctrine of obedience to the loved one. With Chaucer these questions are linked with the discussion of what is true 'gentilesse' or nobility, on which there is a long disquisition in the Wife's *Tale*.

> Crist wole we clayme of hym our gentillesse.

Great possessions and inheritance do not make nobility, for often we see a lord's son do 'shame and vileynye'. Poverty is no disqualification for nobility. God chose to live in poverty when he came into the world, and poverty, though hateful, is good. Age is no disqualification, for both experience and authority command us to respect old age.

The tale is thus subtle and rich in significance. At first, while the character of the narrator is clearly before us, the tone is satirical, and it is women, again, whom the Wife of Bath is made mainly to satirize. Then the tone imperceptibly changes, and the knight is regarded some- what ironically as he gloomily settles in to his wedding night with the old hag who has saved his life. It is she who instructs him in true 'genti- lesse', and her instruction is related to the plot by Chaucer's sharpening of the final dilemma with which she confronts him. In Gower's treat- ment of the same plot the choice is between having the lady beautiful by day or by night. The knight's choice in the Wife's *Tale* is between having the lady poor, old, and ugly, but humble and true; or beautiful with all the risk that beauty may bring. This is a much more interesting problem. When the knight grants the lady sovereignty by allowing her to make the choice herself, she chooses to be fair, and humble and true as well. Having been granted sovereignty she uses it well and returns it. There is the foundation for a perpetual generous exchange.

In the poem there is, too, a genuine mysteriousness and freshness in the glimpse of the fairy ladies dancing 'under a forest side'. They disap- pear when the anxious knight approaches, and he finds only the old hag. Chaucer does not attempt, as Gower does, to go into the details of the enchantment; he knows when to leave well alone. The interest of the plot, its relation with the narrator and with other stories and themes in the *Tales*, the grace, humanity and humour of the telling, make the poem one of Chaucer's best.

—D. S. Brewer, *Chaucer*, 3rd ed. (London: Longman, 1973): pp. 139–41.

MURIEL BOWDEN ON THE WIFE OF BATH'S APPEARANCE

[Muriel Bowden is the author of two books on Chaucer: *A Commentary on the General Prologue to the Canterbury Tales* (1948) and *A Reader's Guide to Geoffrey Chaucer* (1964).]

It is true that Dame Alisoun is conspicuously overdressed on Sundays, but is this not by design? Why should she not let the world see that she is successful enough to warrant fine clothes of good material? Her wearing of such garments stamps her as the most prosperous woman of business in St. Michael-juxta-Bathon, and naturally she takes pleasure "to se, and eek for to be seye" as she later tells us with gusto in her own *Prologue*, and adds that much usage keeps the moths from her beautiful scarlet apparel! We need not believe, then, that Chaucer is exaggerating when he writes of Alisoun's ten-pound "coverchiefs" which were so finely textured ("ful fyne of ground"). The *coverchief* of the Middle Ages was a veil-like structure which was arranged in folds over the head; the coverchief could be simple and light, or elaborate and heavy. The Wife's scarlet hose, also part of her festival attire, are always tightly and neatly drawn ("ful streite ytyed"), and the shoes which complete this imposing costume are of new and supple ("moyste") leather.

The Wife's dress for the pilgrimage, however, is much more sensible. True, her hat is as broad as a shield ("a bokeler or a targe"), but it is firmly placed on her trimly wimpled head; and she is careful enough to wear a protective outer skirt (a "footmantel") about her ample hips, when she rides her "amblere." An ambling horse (often called a pacer today) is one which has been taught to lift two feet together on the same side of its body, making for comfortable riding on a long journey, and is therefore precisely the mount an experienced traveller such as Alisoun would choose. And since Alisoun wears a "paire" of sharp spurs, we know she rides astride, as most women of her class did in Chaucer's time.

The Wife of Bath's orderly and well set-up appearance, as has been suggested, is in keeping with the strong directness of her character. She is one who has always known exactly what she wants and exactly how to get it. She desires, and has obtained importance in her community; good times with gay companions—

> In felaweshipe wel koude she laughe and carpe;

a wide variety of love affairs; and, as we shall hear, the excitements and pleasures of travel. The Wife of Bath leads a systematized life for all its florid quality, and so her bold countenance, "reed of hewe," escapes being blowzy and is attractive in its vigour.

Throughout the years, Dame Alisoun has been, perhaps, most famous—or infamous—for her marital and extra-marital adventures:

> She was a worthy womman al hire lyve:
> Housbondes at chirche dore she hadde fyve,
> Withouten oother compaignye in youthe—
> But thereof nedith nat to speke as nowthe.

Chaucer's contemporaries could not have been as startled as we are by the number of Alisoun's husbands, for, as Dr. Coulton writes, "the extreme promptitude with which the Wife of Bath provided herself with a new husband . . . is characteristically medieval." A woman of any property in the Middle Ages found it as difficult to remain single as the dowerless daughter to marry: no matter how unwilling the woman with even a few possessions might be to enter into a marriage contract, which as a rule was literally just that, a cut-and-dried bargain, some man with a covetous eye upon her worldly goods would compel her, using violent means if necessary, to marry him. If the lady were willing, as Alisoun too plainly always was, it would be unthinkable that she should remain a widow no matter how frequently she might temporarily arrive at that state. Chaucer's audience, therefore, would not have found the fact of the Wife's five husbands astonishing or intrinsically humorous, but they undoubtedly looked forward with a keen relish to hearing the details of Alisoun's management of her various consorts; an Alisoun in any period of history is so obviously born "to han the governance" in wedded life!

But the Alisouns of the medieval world were certainly in the minority; the lot of most women in Chaucer's time was not one of mastery or of freedom. The common sentiment that "woman is man's ruin," was backed by the firm conviction that all females were created as vastly inferior to males. A woman should never strive with her husband, writes the Knight of la Tour Landry, and proceeds to tell the story of the justifiable fate of a wife who dared to place herself on an equal footing with her husband. The latter was so angered by his wife's attempts at "governaunce" that he knocked her down, thus breaking her nose so that her face was permanently "foule blemisshed." Hence, concludes the Knight of la Tour Landry, one sees that a wife ought silently to permit her husband to be the master, "for that is her worshippe." We are reminded by this edifying "ensaumple" that the Wife of Bath has suffered a physical injury for like cause—

> But she was somdel deef, and that was scathe.

We find out later that, after considerable provocation, Alisoun's fifth husband, the "som tyme clerk of Oxenford," in a vain effort to assert his male superiority once struck the intractable Alisoun about the ears so violently that her hearing is now impaired.

Dr. Owst suggests that the ultimate source of the Wife of Bath is the woman in the Book of Proverbs who is "subtil of heart." Fourteenth-century preachers turn again and again to this passage, expanding the interpretation to meet the exigencies of a particular sermon or the homilist's fancy. Too many modern women are "foolish," the sermons say: these women lay snares to entrap men instead of chastely staying at home with their husbands, they talk too much and love gossip, they deck themselves in unseemly finery. One preacher, for example, speaks of "a foolish woman, garrulous and vagrant, impatient out of quiet, not able to keep her feet within the house, now she is without, now in the streets," never constant. And worst of all are the women who will not submissively follow out the wishes of their husbands! But whether Dame Alisoun owes her existence in part to sermon-complaints, or whether the sermon-complaints were brought about because there were enough actual women like Alisoun to warrant the pulpit dissatisfaction, cannot be determined. As Dr. Coulton points out, "In every generation moralists noted with pain the gradual emancipation of ladies from a restraint which had always been excessive, and had often been merely theoretical." Perhaps Chaucer, in creating Alisoun, drew on both homily and the New Woman of his day; whatever the case, his audience must have greeted Alisoun as irresistibly amusing and lifelike.

—Muriel Bowden, *A Commentary on the General Prologue to the Canterbury Tales.* 2nd ed. (New York: Macmillan, 1966): pp. 216–19.

JOHN LAWLOR ON THE VICTORIOUS WIFE OF BATH

[John Lawlor, Professor of English Language and Literature at the University of Keele, is the author of the book *Chaucer*, a critical interpretation of Chaucer as a narrative poet.]

There are, of course, certain tales in which there is a high degree of connection between the tale and the teller, and their case should be instructive. For example, there would be very general agreement about Alice, Wife of Bath. We are told in the General Prologue that 'she was somdel deef'; and when we come to her own autobiographical prologue we learn why, in the blow given her by her fifth husband. Congruity of characterisation and event could not be neater. It is the same with the Pardoner—indeed, more so. A portrait which (uniquely in the General Prologue) opens with outright irony and continues by dilating upon his skill in wooing money from his audiences, prepares us for his stopping to eat and drink while he meditates upon his topic—an ironic curtain-raiser in itself:

> I moot thynke
> Upon som *honest* thyng while that I drynke.

And so we are embarked on another autobiographical prologue, one that reveals the tricks of the trade, and serves to soften up the audience for the grand trick that follows—and all but succeeds. The climax of the 'tale' proper finally disarms suspicion—

> And lo, sires, thus I preche
> And Jhesu Crist, that is our soules leche,
> So graunte yow his pardoun in my male,
> For that is best; I wol yow nat deceyve.

It is at that moment that the never-sleeping salesman strikes:

> But sires, o word forgat I in my tale:
> I have relikes and pardoun in my male,
> As faire as any man in Engelond,
> Which were me yeven by the popes hond.

We need not assume that a long-laid plan is coming to its climax. Skilled opportunism will serve as well as any other explanation: seeing the ring of serious faces around him as he reaches his disarming conclusion, 'I wol yow nat deceyve', the Pardoner strikes home. But whatever we make of the Pardoner's planning, Chaucer's characterisation of him is clear. General Prologue portrait harmonises with autobiographical prologue and the tale itself sustains and in its *dénouement* returns us to the evil eunuch whom we first met. In these two characterisations, then, the Wife of Bath and the Pardoner, we have the highest degree of 'dramatic' relevance—a correspondence between General Prologue portrait and subsequent autobiographical admission which the tale in turn substantiates. But nowhere else in *The Canterbury Tales* do we get this: and the reason that suggests itself is that the Wife of Bath and the Pardoner are two unusually 'fixed' characters, 'fixities and definites', to use a Colerigdean term. If the Pardoner is not quite as Kittredge described him, the one lost soul among the Canterbury pilgrims, he is certainly drawn all one way, without redeeming feature. The crooked Pardoner, or *Quaestor* (who might be a layman authorised for this work), was, we know from many sources, the depth of contemporary evil (and is, we may think, the height of perennial impudence). Where can Liar go in *Piers Plowman*, to seek shelter from the King's officers? Only to the Pardoners who take him in and make him their man. And though successive popes had reprobated the practice, indulgences that purportedly released their purchaser *a pena et a culpa* (release from not merely the punishment but even the guilt of sin) were still in vogue—sufficiently so to stimulate the dazzling paradox that the virtuous Plowman of Langland's *Visio* should be sent one. Piers Plowman goes on to show that potential Christian achievement lies well beyond the scope of ordinary 'indulgences', let alone those fake wares offered by the professional *Quaestors*, those who trade 'pardoun for pens, poundmel aboute'. But there is no changing them in their brazen effrontery. Chaucer's General Prologue ends its portraiture not with any still, sad music of humanity but with the brash din of an 'offertorie' precluding the lucrative harangue:

> Therefore he song the murierly and loude.

The Wife of Bath is another kind of fixed characterization, one peculiarly to medieval taste. Her role is that of unteachable human nature, the voice of unambiguous *pref* over against the many (and sometimes varying) voices of *auctoritee*. Her qualifications to be a fount of wisdom on marriage are given in the General Prologue and amplified in her own autobiographical prologue. She is herself an *auctoritee*—by *pref*. Gordian knots are not meant to be untied:

> Experience, though noon auctoritee
> Were in this world, is right ynogh for me
> To speke of wo that is in mariage.

As such, she occupies a central and honoured place in a holiday poem. She is the Fool of the company, in the traditional acceptance that workaday truth is to be turned upside down. So she is kept in motion. The Clerk—the accredited representative of learned *auctoritee*—bows to her rule. Heaven forbid anyone should look for patient Griseldas nowadays! Much better to forget all 'ernestful matere' and end with a song, to acknowledge the Wife of Bath's 'heigh maistrie', her unquestioned authority in marriage and all things concerned with marriage. The Clerk's capitulation is adroitly phrased. The wife of the story had triumphantly proclaimed over her submissive knight 'Thanne have I gete of yow maistrie'. Now a clerk in his turn yields. Auctoritee defers to experience—but with the ironic reservation that 'elles were it scathe', which implies 'pity it can't be like that'. In this the Clerk has improved upon the lead given by the Friar, impatient to be at the Summoner. He, too, had done mock-reverence before this redoubtable authority:

> 'Dame', quod he, 'God yeve yow right good lyf!
> Ye han heer touched, also moot I thee,
> In scole-matere greet difficultee . . .'

The Friar has seen the drift of her arguments. But, unlike the Clerk, he is minded to keep 'game' and learned matter separate:

> lete auctoritees, on Goddes name,
> To prechyng and to scole eek of clergye.

The Friar's 'game' is all too simple: it is to mock Summoners, as, each and every one,

> a rennere up and doun
> With mandementz for fournicacioun.

The Friar has no time for debate. But the Clerk louts low, and handsomely gives the Wife the victory. Victorious she remains, an undisputed authority on marriage, referred to, one supposes, by Harry Bailly when he glances at those present who could tell a tale if a husband were indiscreet; and openly cited (in disarmingly surrealistic fashion) by a character in the Merchant's Tale. Hers is the rule of unreason. She is carnival Queen for a day that has lasted six centuries.

—John Lawlor, *Chaucer* (London: Hutchinson University Library, 1968): pp. 111–15.

E. Talbot Donaldson on the Prologue and Tale

[E. Talbot Donaldson, Professor Emeritus of English at Indiana University at Bloomington, taught also at Yale, Columbia, and London University. Among his books are *Piers Plowman: The C-Text and Its Poet; Chaucer's Poetry: An Anthology for Modern Reader* (2nd edition, 1975), which serves as the standard for modern Chaucer scholarship and criticism; *Speaking of Chaucer* (1983); and *The Swan at the Well: Shakespeare Reading of Chaucer* (1985).]

The Wife of Bath, always competitive, still competes with Falstaff for the title of the greatest comic character in English literature. Her own ancestry extends back through a literary tradition of antifeminism probably as old as Western culture, though the oldest of her identifiable progenitors is the *Golden Book of Marriages*, written by the Greek Theophrastus, pupil and successor of Aristotle, about 300 B.C. While deriving something also from the Roman Juvenal's viciously antifeminist tract, written about 50 A.D., the Wife probably owes most of her inheritance to St. Jerome's attack (written about 400) on the monk Jovinian, who had rashly undervalued the importance of chastity and thus the gravity of peril women offer men. From later times, one can find her in certain influences of the Englishman Walter Map's witty letter to Rufinus dissuading him from matrimony (written about 1200); and she shares some characteristics of the Old Woman in the second part of the French *Romance of the Rose*, composed about 1280 by Jean de Meun, who constantly amuses himself and his audience with unflattering remarks about women. Her most recent forbear is Eustache Deschamps' *Mirror of Marriage*, a lengthy dissuasion from matrimony that was finished only a few years before the Wife of Bath came to life in Chaucer's poem.

Two salient facts should be noted about this literary ancestry: it generally sees woman at her conceivable worst, and its origin is entirely masculine. The Greek belief that only men were capable of virtue and that women distracted men from its pursuit was adopted by the late Roman stoics, who tried even more rigorously to insulate the virtuous man from the commitment to life that relations with women entail. The latter tradition was in turn adopted by the early propagandists for Christian monastacism, who tended to regard the other sex as the worst of the temptations offered by the world they had renounced. The result of this long tradition was that by Chaucer's time a notion of woman as a kind of monster enjoyed an authority and respectability which made it seem valid despite anything a man might, in his everyday life, observe to the contrary. It is this curious traditional version of truth about woman that Chaucer decided to put to the test in his fiction.

The Wife of Bath's mission, then, is to summarize in her own personality everything that had been said against women for hundreds of years—to write Q.E.D. to a proposition that the centuries had been laboring on. One supposes that when he first though of her Chaucer was possessed of the happy and mischievous idea of forcing the reader to compare the Wife, representing woman in her traditionally lecherous, traditionally avaricious, traditionally domineering, traditionally pragmatic form, with women as the reader knew them: the Wife would be placed before her ink-stained perpetuators and be allowed to say, "You made me what I am today: I hope you're satisfied." Such a plan shows the characteristic double-edge of Chaucerian satire: the creators of this tradition, and contemporary men who professed to believe it, are satirized because the character is a monstrous perversion of what experience shows; but women are satirized too, because in many of her characteristics, inextricably interwoven with the monstrosities, the Wife of Bath is precisely what experience teaches. Chaucer was able here—as so often elsewhere—to have it both ways.

But while this highly distorted concept of womanhood is superbly realized in the Wife of Bath, something better is also realized. As she goes on talking, her traditional lechery, avarice, wilfulness, and pragmatism become woven into a complex of human character that is of a different order from the comparatively negative satirical theme. Her explanations of why she felt entitled to a multiplicity of husbands and how, by deceit and shrewishness, she managed them for her own profit are—despite their grossness—the significant probings of an individual trying to live happily in a world governed by rules that even the most aware of women can only imperfectly understand. If the Wife of Bath has not wholly won the game, she has by no means capitulated. There remains for her the fun she has had in handling her men and competing with them for the mastery—the fun she has had in life itself. It is this motif that comes to dominate her Prologue as it nears the end. The Wife ceases to be an enormously funny parody of a woman invented by woman-haters, ceases even to be a woman fascinating for her intense individuality, ceases in a way to be a woman at all, and becomes instead a high and gallant symbol of a humanity in which weakness and fortitude are inextricably mingled. In the passage in which she surveys her youth with both regret and blessing for what has passed she seems to enlarge the boundaries of human consciousness so that mankind itself becomes more vital because of her. If the Wife of Bath's Prologue were the only literature to survive between 1200 and 1600 one might say that in her character the Renaissance sprang from the Middle Ages.

The *Wife of Bath's Tale* demonstrates the happiest aspects of her character. In what was probably a less developed form she was assigned the tale now told by the Shipman, which illustrates the supposedly basic feminine attributes of avarice and lechery. The present story illustrates a more interesting theme, her desire to dominate the male, along with the corollary—inevitable to the Wife—that female dominance brings happiness to marriage. Chaucer has adapted a popular story (which appears in contemporary romance and in a later ballad, as well as in John Gower's *Confessio Amantis*) in such a way as to heighten the Wife's thesis. In the analogues the story is handled in a different style, its real point being to demonstrate the courtesy of the hero, who weds the hag uncomplainingly and treats her as if she were the fairest lady in the land; in two versions the knight is Sir Gawain, the most courteous of Arthur's followers, who promises to marry her not in order to save his own life but his king's. The lady's transformation is thus a reward of virtue. In Chaucer the polite knight becomes a convicted rapist who keeps his vow only under duress and in the sulkiest possible manner. The reformation of such unlikely material is the ultimate tribute the Wife could pay to woman's ability to accomplish good if she is allowed to dominate.

The tale is in other respects entirely the Wife's. The wit with which she pays off the Friar, who has the temerity to interrupt her, while at the same time getting her own story under way, is what we have learned to expect from her. So also is the digression on feminine desires and weaknesses which leads her to give the story of Midas— in which Midas' queen is substituted for the barber of the original Ovidian version. Criticism is sometimes directed against the hag's long sermon to her young husband, on the grounds that it reveals an unexpected delicacy in the Wife's character, but behind all the masculine forcefulness of the Wife's Prologue there lies a highly feminine sensitivity. Finally, it need hardly be said that there is a suggestive parallel between the hag and the Wife of Bath, both of whom have wed husbands far younger than they; but the hag, of course, is able to regain her beauty. In her story the Wife is able to make the rules that govern the world, as she has not been able to do in her life. Pathos, however, must not be allowed to carry the day: the coarse vigor of the Wife's final benediction restores the full robustness of her personality. She will, one may be sure, always be as sturdily merry as before.

> —E. Talbot Donaldson, ed., *Chaucer's Poetry: An Anthology for the Modern Reader* (New York: The Ronald Press Co., 1975), pp. 913–16.

DONALD HOWARD ON WHAT THE TALE REVEALS ABOUT THE WIFE OF BATH

[Donald R. Howard was Professor of English at the John Hopkins University and also Stanford University. He is the author of *Writers and Pilgrims: Medieval Pilgrimage Narratives* and *Chaucer, His Life, His Works, His World.* He died in March 1987.]

It is easy to understand why her opinions about sovereignty generate a "discussion of marriage," but the tale she tells really undercuts her feminist views, reveals something about her we could only have suspected, something she doesn't know herself. Freud is said to have told Marie Bonaparte, "The great question that has never been answered and which I have not yet been able to answer, despite my thirty years of research into the feminine soul, is 'What does a woman want?' " Chaucer managed to understand on instinct something about this question, and he gave expression to that understanding by having the Wife herself pose the question and answer it unwittingly. In one of her digressions she has said why she loved her fifth husband best:

We women han, if that I shall nat lie,
In this mattere a queynte fantasie;
Waite what thing we may nat lightly have,
Thereafter wol we cry all day and crave.
Forbede us thing, and that desiren we;
Press on us fast, and thanne wol we flee.

Her tale, if it is an exemplum, exemplifies this point. But it comes closer to being a "queynte fantasie" than an exemplum—a wish-fulfillment fantasy in which an ugly old hag is transformed into a beautiful young girl, a handsome husband provided, male dominance surrendered, and a happy marriage established. What more could any woman want? The Wife's notion in her prologue that women want most what they cannot have is narrowed down in her tale: her "lusty bachelor," guilty of rape, can save his life by going on a quest to find out "what thing it is that women most desiren." She provides a compendium of possible answers to the question, the diverse opinions the knight hears in his quest concluding with a tale from Ovid—an exemplum within an exemplum; when he meets the hag, she demands that he fulfill the next thing she asks of him, then whispers the truth in his ear. At court he reports his findings, and all agree he is right:

Women desiren to have sovereigntee
As well over hir husbond as hir love,
And for to been in maistrie him above.
This is your most desire ...

Given the dependency status of women in medieval society, this bears out the Wife's notion that women want most "what thing we may nat lightly have." True, she ends asking short life for husbands that won't be governed by their wives and for "old and angry niggardes of dispence," and prays that women get "Husbondes meeke, young, and fresh abedde" plus the grace to outlive them. But this is a coda; the tale itself has a surprise ending. When the subdued husband and the transformed hag are united, we learn at the end:

And she obeyed him in every thing
That mighte do him plesance or liking.

The wife's obedience here is comparable to the "happy ending" of the Wife's prologue: the fifth husband, having submitted to her, never had any more trouble. She says:

> . . . I was to him as kinde
> As any wife from Denmark to Inde
> And also trewe, and so was he to me.

What the Wife really wants, and what she unwittingly suggests women want, is a *token* submission on the part of the husband— they want the "maistry" in marriage, but when they have it they want not to exercise it. It is an ambivalent wish typical of human nature, and as true of men as of women. We want to be dependent and independent both, and much of the time we don't know what we want. Probably happiness in marriage, or in any interpersonal relations, depends on the sorting-out of these conflicting desires; if there is such a thing as mutuality in human relationships it must be based on an *entente cordiale* between the desire for omnipotence and the desire for love. The Wife in her roundabout way gets at such a fundamental truth about human nature that the rest of the "marriage group" seems like sound and fury. She diverts the discussion from perfection to "maistry," and from "maistry" to what a woman wants. You can't read any of the other tales without thinking about what you've learned from the Wife, that neither men or women fully know what they want and most often want it both ways. The structure of the group has the quality of a digression which trails away from the heart of the matter.

—Donald Howard, *The Idea of* The Canterbury Tales (Berkeley: University of California Press, 1976): pp. 253–55.

DONALD HOWARD ON THE WIFE OF BATH AND CHAUCER'S MARRIAGE

[In this extract from *Chaucer: His Life, His Works, His World* (1987), Donald R. Howard examines Chaucer's marriage and the death of his wife in a discussion of the Wife of Bath.]

Chaucer had been working on *The Canterbury Tales* for about a year when his wife, Philippa, died, in the twenty-first year of their marriage. She was in her middle forties. Of her death nothing is known. She drops from the pages of history by virtue of dropping from the pages of the Issue Rolls: Chaucer collected, as he customarily did, the payment of her annuity on June 18, 1387. The next payment, due the following November, was not made, nor any payment after. Where or how she died is beyond conjecture. As we've said, she was probably with her sister Katherine in Lincolnshire. John of Gaunt was in Spain, the Duchess Costanza with him. In July Chaucer was sent to Calais on the king's business, in August to Dartford on a commission investigating the abduction of a young woman. It is hard to imagine that he would have been sent on such commissions in the first months of mourning, so her death must have come in the autumn.

We do not know if Chaucer was with Philippa when she died, nor even what terms they were on in the last years of their marriage. Unless the Cecily Champain affair, which can hardly have been kept secret, were altogether innocent, their relations were probably strained. So when we come to the sequence in *The Canterbury Tales* that Kittredge called "Chaucer's discussion of marriage," which begins with the Wife's expressions of nostalgia and regret, not to say of her wish for a sixth husband, it's hard to escape the conclusion that this striking literary conception was in part occasioned by Philippa Chaucer's death. Chaucer was suddenly a widower; after a time he was thinking of marrying again. In a poem he wrote to his friend Scogan (circa 1393), he reveals with good humor that he is beginning to see himself as beyond the age of love and marriage; and with humor but here with a sharp edge, that he had decided against remarriage. Experience will teach his friend not to fall into the "trap of wedding," for it is hard, he declares, to be "bond"—to be enslaved. And he cites the Wife of Bath as an authority!

The "marriage group," as this sequence of tales is generally called, could have been an outlet for very complicated emotions. In it he could look back with regret, perhaps remorse, upon his marriage and with uncertainty toward his future. That he projected his widower's feelings on a female character is not especially surprising; it helped distance those feelings, of whose expression he may have remained quite unaware. Medieval poetry was never knowingly used for "self-expression," but the best poetry has in it—witness Dante— the deepest feelings of the writer, and such feelings are by nature personal. Chaucer had the makings of the Wife and her prologue at hand in the long monologue of the Duenna in the *Roman de la Rose*. And there *were* Englishwomen like the Wife who ran prosperous businesses and had a cheeky independence. Perhaps trying to see his own marriage through his dead wife's eyes, trying to assess some of his own shortcomings as a husband, he hit upon the remarkable notion of a garrulous woman from the merchant class who knew what the church fathers said about women and marriage, knew the Church's antifeminist lore and its position about "perfection" in matters of sex and marriage, and was prepared to offer a rebuttal. How could any medieval woman know all that? A woman like the Wife of Bath might have great native intelligence and a retentive memory, and some women of this class could read—but the church fathers, who wrote in Latin? Yet she could know them *if her husband read to her aloud.* He imagined a characteristic medieval *florilegium* composed of such writings, and then imagined a young husband, the Wife's fifth, once an Oxford clerk (he has the cliché clerk's name "Jankyn") who had such a "Book of Wicked Wives" and took a perverse delight in reading to her from it.

Chaucer had the Wife of Bath begin her discourse with a question that was on *his* mind: Is it better to remarry or not to remarry? The Church's answer was that there were "grades" of perfection and in the sexual sphere chastity was highest. If one married, it was better to marry once, and, if the spouse died, never again, a state called "widowhood." Beyond that, it was allowable to marry more than once, but to do so put you lower on the ladder of perfection. The Wife is in this lowest state, which she embraces with a certain questionable gusto—"Welcome the sixth!" Chaucer was in the intermediate state, "widowhood," and there may have been times when he thought, "Welcome the second." He has the Wife summarize quite accurately the doctrines he must himself have been mulling over (it is plain he had been reading Saint Jerome): the saints are specially called to the highest state, and we should not envy them. We are only counseled to be perfect, not commanded, but we are commanded to "go forth and multiply" ("That gentle text can I well understand!" cries the Wife). There could be no virgins if no seed were sown. Nature gave us organs of generation to this purpose, and we are expected to "pay the marriage debt." Yet the Wife, championing "engendrure," never says anything about her having children, which suggests that she was barren. This could indicate certain feelings at a deep level that Chaucer had about himself, feelings of emptiness or futility or unfulfillment. On the other hand, he may have kept silent about whether the Wife had children for the same reason he did so with respect to Criseyde, to avoid those aspects of a woman's experience a man finds hard to imagine. And too, if his son Thomas was really the bastard son of John of Gaunt and Philippa, and his son Lewis was his bastard son by Cecily Champain, perhaps the subject of children was better not raised.

In line 154 of her prologue the Wife changes the subject and never returns to this question of remarriage and "perfection." Unless Chaucer meant to pick it up later in the Second Nun's Tale, which depicts a chaste marriage dedicated to the Church, the subject is permanently dropped. The Wife turns to her second question, which must also have been Chaucer's: What kind of a marriage does one want? And here she sets forth her thesis that the woman should have the upper hand in marriage and the man have the "tribulacioun." This gets an immediate rise from the Pardoner; claiming he was about to wed a wife but now thinks better of it, he eggs her on. She begins with her first three husbands, who were old and rich, and whom she harassed for their putative slanders against women— which produces a remarkable and very funny compendium of antifeminist notions. There follows the bitter story of her fourth husband, who deserted her. And yet she interrupts this harsh recital with those nostalgic, yearning lines that shimmer with her indomitable *joie de vivre* and her toughness—some of Chaucer's best lines, which must express a feeling he knew, perhaps about the earlier years of his marriage before things went awry:

> But, Lord Crist! whan that it remembreth me
> Upon my youth and on my jollitee,
> It tickleth me about myn hearte roote.
> Unto this day it dooth myn hearte boote
> That I have had my world as in my time.

Her tale ends with the story of the young fifth husband, Jankyn, over whom at last she gains what she calls "the governance of house and land, and of his tongue, and of his hand also." After they fought and she pretended to be dead, she made him burn his book on the spot. And after his submission, she says, they fought no more: she was always kind to him and true, and so was he to her. The implication is that if the husband submits to the Wife's sovereignty, the result is mutuality, a marriage as between equals.

The "Marriage Group" is the most focused of the groups of tales, and it begins with such a flourish, moves with such dramatic intensity, and ends so ambiguously, that one can imagine it came to Chaucer all at once as a fully integrated concept. He envisaged the Wife's whirlwind discourse, her five husbands, Jankyn and his book, their fight, her deaf ear, her argument for women's "sovereigntee," and the description of male reactions that would follow. He wrote the description of her in the General Prologue, or added to it her deafness in one ear, and he found for her a tale—the tale of the ugly old hag who knows what women really want—more appropriate and far more revealing than the one he had originally assigned to her, which became the Shipman's.

—Donald Howard, *Chaucer: His Life, His Works, His World* (New York: E.P. Dutton, 1987): pp. 428–31.

HAROLD BLOOM ON THE WIFE OF BATH AND FALSTAFF

[Harold Bloom is Sterling Professor of the Humanities at Yale University and Berg Professor of English at New York University. He is the author of more than twenty books, including the best-selling *The Western Canon* (1994), and *The Anxiety of Influence* (1973), which sets forth Professor Bloom's theory of the literary relationships between the great writers and their predecessors.]

Despite her five late husbands, she appears to be childless and says nothing about the matter. Where she does cross into opposition to the ideology of the medieval church is on the issue of dominance in marriage. Her firm belief in female sovereignty is the center of her rebellion, and I dissent from Howard when he says that her tale "undercuts her feminist views, reveals something about her we could only have suspected, something she doesn't even know herself." In this view, the wife wants only an outward or verbal submission on the husband's part, but that is to underestimate the Wife's own share of Chaucerian irony. Two lines do not a tale make, nor do they undo eight hundred lines of passionate prologue: "And she obeyed him in every thing / That mighte doon him plesance or lyking."

I take it that the Wife intends the phrase "in every thing" to be exclusively sexual. The lines directly follow one in which the husband kisses the wife a thousand times in a row, and the Wife of Bath's idea of what might give a man pleasure is rather monolithic. She wants sovereignty all right, everywhere except in bed, as her inevitable sixth husband is going to learn. As she had told us, her first three husbands were good, rich, and old, whereas the fourth and fifth were young and troublesome. The fourth, having dared to take a mistress, suffered the just fate of being tormented to death by her; and the fifth, half her age, deafened her by boxing her ears, after she had ripped pages out of the antifeminist book he insisted upon reading to her. When he yielded at last, burned the book, and resigned sovereignty to her, they lived happily together, but not ever after. Chaucer's ironic implication is that the ferociously lustful Wife wore out the beloved fifth husband, even as she had used up the first four.

Her fellow pilgrims clearly understand what the Wife is saying. Whether the reader is male or female, only tone deafness or revulsion from life could resist the Wife's most sublime moments of yearning and self-celebration. In the midst of her account of her fourth husband, she muses upon her love of wine and its close relation to her love of love, and then suddenly cries out,

But Lord Crist! whan that it remembreth me	[I think]
Upon my yowthe, and on my jolitee,	[gaiety]
It tikleth me aboute myn herte rote.	[tickles/heart's root]
Unto this day it dooth myn herte bote	[good]
That I have had my world as in my tyme.	
But age, allas! that al wol evenyme,	[poison]
Hath me biraft my beautee and my pith.	[bereft of/vigor]
Lat go, farewel! the devel go therwith!	[Let it go]
The flour is gone, ther is namore to telle:	
The bren, as best I can, now moste I selle;	[brans or husks]
But yet to be right mery wol I fonde.	[try]

There are no fresh revelations here; nothing that will help complete the scope and structure of the *Canterbury Tales*. These eleven lines mix the Wife's memory and desire, while acknowledging that time has transfigured her. If there is a passage in Chaucer that breaks through his own ironies, it is this one, in which all the irony belongs to time, invincible enemy of all heroic vitalists. Against that irony, the still heroic Wife of Bath sets the grandest of all her lines: "That I have had my world as in my tyme." "*My* time" is the triumph; reduced to husks as her vitality may be, the true pith of the woman abides in her Falstaffian high spirits. Ruefulness abounds and authenticates her realistic sense of loss: the rancidity or an aging lust may not be far away, but her understanding that only deliberate cheerfulness is appropriate for her constitutes the secular or experiential wisdom that completes her critique of the churchly ideals that might condemn her. Chaucer, feeling old indeed in his later fifties, has given her an eloquence worthy of both the character and her creator.

Does the Wife of Bath change in the course of her long confession of a prologue? Chaucerian irony is hardly a mode by which change is represented. We listen to the Wife of Bath's monologue; so do the Pilgrims. Does she overhear herself? We are very moved to hear that she has had the world in her time. Is she not moved also? She does not have the brilliantly schooled self-awareness of the Pardoner, who generally is blind only to the effect that he has on himself. The Wife's deepest affinity to Falstaff is that she appreciates her own appreciation of herself. She has no desire to change and therefore manifests throughout her prologue a spirited resistance to aging and so to the final form of change, death. What does alter her is the quality of her high spirits, which transmute from natural exuberance into highly self-conscious vitalism.

That change, as far as I can tell, is not treated ironically by Chaucer, perhaps because, unlike so many of his scholars, he has too great an affection for his remarkable creation and allows her to appeal directly to the reader. Her deliberate cheerfulness differs from forced heartiness; the nearest analogue to it is the buoyancy of Sir John Falstaff, who has been even more maligned by scholarly critics. Falstaff's wit does not decline in *Henry IV, Part Two*, but we feel there is a darkening in him as his rejection by Hal gradually approaches. The Falstaffian gusto is still there, but the gaiety begins to acquire an edge, as though the will to live takes on a touch of an ideology of vitalism. The Wife of Bath and Falstaff both become less like the Panurge of Rabelais. They are still bearers of the Blessing, and both still cry out for more life, but they have learned that there is no time without boundaries, and they accept the new role of being antagonists, fighting for their waning share of the Blessing. Although the wife has a powerful command of rhetoric and a dangerous wit, she cannot compete with Falstaff in these regards. Her rugged consciousness of a diminishment in vitality and her strong will to maintain her high spirits are closer analogues to Shakespeare's greatest comic character.

The Wife and Falstaff are ironists, early and late, and they found their authority upon their self-confident personalities, as Donaldson has noted. With Don Quixote, Sancho Panza, and Panurge they make up a company or family devoted to the order of play, as opposed to the order of society or of the organized spirit. What the order of play confers, within its strict limits, is freedom, the inner freedom of ceasing to be badgered by one's own superego. I take it that this is why one reads Chaucer and Rabelais, Shakespeare and Cervantes. For a space, the superego ceases to whack one for supposedly harboring aggressivity. The rhetorical drive of the Wife and Falstaff is nothing if not aggressive, but the pragmatic aim is freedom: from the world, from time, from the moralities of state and church, from whatever in the self impedes the self's triumphs of self-expression. Even some admirers of the Wife of Bath and Falstaff persist in calling them solipsists; but egocentricity is not solipsism. The Wife and Falstaff are perfectly aware of neighbors and the sun, but very few who come near them interest us much, compared to these enchanted vitalists.

Many scholars have pointed to the equivocal relation both the Wife and Falstaff have to the text in First Corinthians in which Paul calls on Christians to persist in their vocation. The Wife's version is, "In such a state as God hath cleped us / I wol persever: I nam not precious," and Falstaff both echoes and outdoes her: "Why, Hal, 'tis my vocation, Hal, 'tis no sin for a man to labor in his vocation." In mocking Paul, the Wife and Falstaff are not being primarily impious. As wits they are both disenchanters, but they remain believers. The Wife deftly keeps reminding the godly that perfection is not required of her, while Falstaff is haunted by the fate of Dives the glutton. Falstaff is more anxiety-ridden than the Wife, but she has not suffered the kind of misfortune of regarding the future Henry V as a kind of adopted son. Being Shakespeare's rather than Chaucer's, Falstaff undergoes more change by internalization than the Wife is capable of experiencing. Both characters listen to themselves, but only Falstaff consistently overhears himself.

—Harold Bloom, *The Western Canon* (New York: Harcourt Brace, 1994): pp. 116–19.

Thematic Analysis of the
Pardoner's Prologue

There are two parts to the Pardoner's story: the Prologue, 164 lines, and the tale, 505 lines long, and they work together splendidly.

The Pardoner's prologue further develops the character that Chaucer introduced in the General Prologue. The practices of the pardoners, of selling pardons for cash, were the subject of moralists and satirists. The Pardoner in his prologue displays impressive self-awareness and he congratulates himself for his criminally vicious characteristics. That provokes comic elements as well as it horrifies.

The Pardoner indicates the theme of his prologue: *Radix malorum est cupiditas* ("Avarice is the root of Evil"). Whenever he preaches, the Pardoner says, his text is always the same: he preaches about the root of evil, which is avarice. But before that he announces where he has come from, then he shows all his certificates and his papal bulls. During the sermon, in order to color his speech and stir devotion, he drops in a few Latin words. He also, as he says, brings out his glass cases with relics and explains the magical power of the shoulder bone of one of Jacob's sheep, which dipped in a well can cure cows, sheep, or oxen, and can even help cure jealousy.

Then he invites those who are free of guilt to make an offering in God's name. By these tricks he earns a hundred marks a year. He admits that his only purpose is gain and that he doesn't care about correcting anyone's sins. He is aware that some sermons are preached from a motive to please or to flatter, and to thereby gain advancement by hypocrisy; others are preached out of vanity or malice. If he doesn't attack those who offended him by some other means, he'll sting them with his sharp tongue in a sermon, so that they cannot escape his slander. Although he never names his enemy, everyone knows perfectly well from his hints who he is talking about. He knows what to say about avarice because it is the very vice that he practices. At the end of the sermon he tells a moral tale every time, and he will tell one to the pilgrims on their journey to Canterbury. ❀

Thematic Analysis of the
Pardoner's Tale

Before he actually begins his tale, the Pardoner gives a highly effective sermon on drunkenness, gluttony, swearing, and gambling. He shows that he definitely knows how to work upon his audience's emotions, in comparison with the pious Parson, who probably put everybody to sleep.

His story is about three revellers who swear eternal brotherhood to one another, and who are in search to kill the false traitor, Death. They give their frightful oaths: Death to Death, if only they can get hold of him. On their way in search of Death, they haven't yet gone half a mile when they meet a poor old man, all muffled up to the eyes. He tells them that he has walked from here to India, but that he can't find a man who will exchange his youth for his age, and that not even Death will take his life.

They insist that he tell them where they can find Death, and he tells them to go to the oak tree in the grove at the end of the road. They set off running at once and come to the tree where they find five newly minted golden florins (coins). They stop searching for Death and sit down full of joy at the sight of the treasure. The worst of the three suggests they draw lots, and that the one who draws the longest straw will run to the town to bring bread and wine while the other two take care of the treasure. It falls on the youngest to go. The other two plan to slay the youngest when he comes back. When he returns they slay him on the spot, but as they drink the wine that the youngest thoughtfully has poisoned, they also perish.

The Pardoner finishes his story, but then asks his fellow pilgrims to kiss his relics for sixpence and receive his pardon. The host, Harry Bailly, cries out that he would rather have his ballocks than his holy souvenirs. The Pardoner eschews further comment. ❀

Critical Views on the
Pardoner's Prologue and Tale

CHARLES MUSCATINE ON CHAUCERIAN IRONY

[Charles Muscatine is Professor of English at the University of California, Berkeley. He is the author of *Chaucer Tradition and the French.*]

In *The Pardoner's Tale* the mixed style is an instrument of the remarkable characterisation which finally dominates the poem. It is the very style of the Pardoner, who is the only pilgrim dramatically given literary powers comparable to those of Chaucer himself. The depth of the characterisation depends in part on the fact that in the Pardoner's mixed style, unlike in Chaucer's, the speaker is somehow made to fail in his irony. He turns out to be hardly humorous at all; his style rather deepens the curious blend of the grotesque and the pathetic already to be found in his portrait.

The stylistic components of the tale are easy to discern. The tale (with its prologue) is a dramatic monologue—that of Jean de Meun's character Faus-Semblant, but technically much more skilful. Within the dramatic monologue is a real medieval sermon, with its homiletic realism, its rhetoric and its *exempla*. On this level we are on familiar Chaucerian ground. The high-flown rhetoric of the sermon, in the context of the self-revelation of the monologue, produces a mock-effect which satirises the canned fireworks of the professional preachers. Chaucer underlines this effect by making the rhetorical outbursts glaringly ornamental, so that our attention is transferred from the meaning of the speech to the manipulations of the speaker. One can almost hear the Pardoner simulating the tears of St. Paul:

> The apostel weping seith ful pitously,
> 'Ther walken manye of which you toold have I—
> I seye it now wepyng, with pitous voys—
> They that have been enemys of Cristes croys,
> Of which the end is death, wombe is hir god!'
> O wombe! O bely! O stynkyng cod,
> Fulfilled of dong and of corrupcioun!

John Speirs has well pointed out the conjunction in this sermon of 'vigorous popular speech with scholastic phraseology', of 'coarseness and . . . metaphysics'. The realistic imagery here is inherited along with the learning from the ascetic-homiletic tradition, with its graphic descriptions of the fleshliness that must be condemned. But Chaucer makes it too vivid to remain simply satiric. It is presented with such a 'thunderous overcharge . . . of feeling', Speirs points out, that it characterises the Pardoner as being unconsciously 'both half-horrified and half-fascinated' by his subject. This is going beyond the ordinary Chaucerian irony; it makes the sermon both more ironic and less ironic than the Pardoner knows. His fascination raises his cynicism to a grotesque new power, while his horror reduces it to pathos. The sermon's great terminal *exemplum* of the three revellers who sought Death similarly breaks through the bonds of a simple satire on sermons. It is too convincing. The resulting stretch in the characterisation between redeeming sincerity and outright monstrosity is underlined stylistically in the sequence beginning at line 895. The whole gamut of Chaucer's styles can be found here in twenty lines, from the terrible rhetorical outcry, through the 'broches, spoones, rynges' of domestic realism, to the touching special simplicity of 'And lo, sires, thus I preche'.

The juxtaposition of tales to each other and to the dramatic frame of the pilgrimage is the largest counter of Chaucer's style. It is the largest manifestation of what we can see in *The Canterbury Tales* from the mixed idiom up: Chaucer's endless interest in comparisons and relationships. 'How shall the world be served?' is the question he asks. The great range of values and attitudes expressed in these tales represent his grand confrontation of it. The comedy and the tolerant irony, the relativism, the necessity to perceive: these are the answer implied by his mixed style.

—Charles Muscatine, "*The Canterbury Tales:* Style of the Man and Style of the Work," *Chaucer and Chaucerians*, ed. D.S. Brewer (Tuscaloosa, Ala.: University of Alabama Press, 1966): pp. 112–13.

[E. Talbot Donaldson, Professor Emeritus of English at Indiana University at Bloomington, taught also at Yale, Columbia, and London University. Among his books are *Piers Plowman: The C-Text and Its Poet; Chaucer's Poetry: An Anthology for the Modern Reader* (2nd edition, 1975), which serves as the standard for modern Chaucer scholarship and criticism; *Speaking of Chaucer* (1983) and *The Swan at the Well: Shakespeare Reading of Chaucer* (1985).]

The Pardoner, like the Wife of Bath, owes something to the continuation of the *Roman de la Rose*, which thus contributed both to the most vital and to the most repellently sterile of Chaucer's characters. In the French poem Jean de Meun introduces a character named False-Seeming, a professional hypocrite who pretends a holiness that he possesses not at all. By way of making an apology for his way of life, False-Seeming explains, with the utmost candor and the greatest pride in his own cleverness, the various guises his hypocrisy assumes. This situation, in which a hypocrite attempts to justify himself by revealing the full truth, provides Chaucer with the essential framework for the Pardoner's prologue.

It also gives him the first of a series of paradoxes that are developed in the character and in his tale. Paradox in Chaucer's poetry, as in Milton's, often has two opposed functions: when applied to the mysteries of the Christian religion (the Virgin Mother, the God-Man) it expresses the superiority of the divine to the laws that govern nature; applied to human beings it may express the animality of man's nature in his farthest remove from the divinity of his creator. This is certainly true of the Pardoner, who while he converts grace—God's great gift to man—into cash for his own pocket, simultaneously perverts the divine system of salvation in order to accomplish his own damnation. Fittingly enough, he eventually is entrapped by the paradox of his own nature. The *General Prologue* makes it clear that the Pardoner is a eunuch. To the medieval mind, which liked to find in the visible world the patterns of the invisible, this lack of manliness would suggest the barrenness of the Pardoner's spirit, and it is this condition that causes, in the visible world of the pilgrimage, the punishment that he seems to be doomed to in the world of the spirit. The Pardoner has, from his first appearance, presented himself as a virile, gay lad, a jolly good fellow, an accomplished wencher. When he enters the scene in the *General Prologue* he is singing a love song—though an ironically wistful one; he has the temerity to interrupt the Wife of Bath, that great proponent of sexual love, in order to publicize his virility; when the Host, addressing the Physician, swears by Saint Runnion—apparently a reference to sexuality—the Pardoner must needs repeat the oath; he seems pleased, in the same passage, to be called *bel ami*, a phrase that still means "lover" in Modern French; and finally, he boast that he will have a jolly wench in every town. In view of the evident facts of the case, all this is the rankest hypocrisy. As the only hypocrisy that survives the candor of the Pardoner's self-revelation it probably is the explanation for his candor, for men often believe that they can best keep a shameful secret by seeming to reveal the whole truth about themselves.

But the Pardoner's secret is, of course, a secret only to himself: at any rate Chaucer the pilgrim guessed it at once. But as long as the secret remains unspoken the Pardoner dwells securely in his own delusion, so that the secret remains valid for him. Yet at the end of his frightening story he wantonly imperils—and destroys—the fragile structure on which his self-confidence depends. Whatever his reasons—avarice, good-fellowship, humor—he concludes his sermon with an offer to sell his pardon to the pilgrims even after all he has told about his own fraudulence. Ironically he picks the worst possible victim, that rough, manly man who might be supposed to have a natural antipathy for the unmasculine Pardoner. The insult to the Host's intelligence is the first and last failure of the Pardoner's intelligence, for the Host's violently obscene reaction reveals the Pardoner's secret. Thereupon every man whose clever tongue has seemed to give him control of every situation is reduced to furious silence.

THE PARDONER'S TALE

The *Pardoner's Tale* is a sample of the sermons with which the Pardoner frightens his congregations into the Christian generosity that makes him rich. Although the story proper illustrates his accustomed text, "Avarice is the root of evil," the introductory lines are a highly emotive discussion of drunkenness, gluttony, swearing, and gambling (with a few glances at lechery). These latter are, to be sure, practiced by the young men whom avarice is in the story ultimately to destroy, but the Pardoner's choice of them for his rhetoric doubtless depends on the fact that they are the sins that can be made to sound most exciting. Since the sermon was one of the main sources of entertainment for the Middle Ages, the preacher generally entertained while he taught, and nothing is easier to dramatize successfully to an uneducated audience than riotous living. Furthermore, it is characteristic of the riotous-living Pardoner's sense of irony that he should here too, as with avarice, inveigh against the very vices he himself practices. He privately delights in his own experience with these vices: there is something gloatingly cynical in his description of a drunken dice-game, so knowingly graphic as to exceed the limits of art. But while the Pardoner may be having his secret laugh, he does not cease to work upon his audience's emotions with every lurid detail that a morbid imagination can provide.

The story itself is one of the most impressive ventures into the supernatural that English literature affords. It is a very old story indeed, probably having its origin in the primitive animism of the East, although in the Pardoner's mouth it becomes an anecdote of contemporary Europe. The plot in which three revelers set out to find death find him in the gold that has made them forget the object of their search gives Chaucer ample opportunity for grim irony. This develops mostly through the speeches of the participants in the story, who are constantly saying far more than they think they are. The naturalism of the dialogue increases by contrast the terror of the supernatural forces that are effortlessly accomplishing their end. For instance, in the monologue of the strange old man who directs the youths to their death, the ultimate mysteries of human life are treated with the familiarity that we accord homely, everyday things. And Death in the end turns out to be someone who, if not a rural bully dwelling in the next village, is equally close at hand. Out of the miasma that hangs invisible just above the heads of the revelers, Death reaches with a sure hand to claim those who had so arrogantly started out to slay him. Nevertheless, despite the strong aura of the supernatural, the entire action is restricted to a purely natural sequence of events.

The ending Chaucer has assigned to the Pardoner himself makes his exemplum even more brilliant. The man who, like the revelers in his story, seems so firmly in control of his destiny, has in his sermon eloquently demonstrated that avenging powers dwell close to a man's own home. If it is not supernatural, it is at least an ironic destiny working through his own nature that impels the Pardoner to provoke his own social destruction among the pilgrims.

—E. Talbot Donaldson, ed. *Chaucer's Poetry: An Anthology for the Modern Reader* (New York: The Ronald Press Co., 1975): pp. 927–30.

DONALD HOWARD ON THE PARDONER AS EXTRAORDINARY PERFORMER

[Donald Howard was Professor of English at the John Hopkins University and also Stanford University. He is the author of *Writers and Pilgrims: Medieval Pilgrimage Narratives* and *Chaucer, His Life, His Works, His World*. He died in March 1987.]

For Chaucer makes us know the Pardoner better than the Pardoner knows himself. He is proud. The delight he takes in his own skill and success is contagious. His hands and tongue go so "yerne," he proclaims, that it is a joy to see. He makes a great point of the financial rewards. He is pleased with the props and bits of stage business he has worked up—the "bulls" he shows, our leige lord's seal on his patent, the spicy words of Latin he speaks "To saffron with my predicacioun," and the relics, his favorite "gaude." He takes childlike delight in this effectiveness, for he is at pains to remind us that he *can* "stir hem to devocioun," can make them "soore to repente." This is "nat my principal entente," he adds, for he takes equal pleasure in his guile:

> For though myself be a full vicious man,
> A moral tale yet I you telle can.

That is what shocks us most: he is proud of his own evil, so much so that he cannot keep from boasting of it. At the end he cannot resist a tour de force of the swindler's art.

He is condescending. The poor simple folk he dupes become in his eyes the object of a contemptuous derision. They are the "lewed peple" who "loven tales olde":

> I stonde like a clerk in my pulpet,
> And whan the lewed peple is down yset,
> I preche so as ye han herd before.

For him they are a mass (he uses the singular verb) whom he can treat like a great draffsack—he even absolves them in a lump at the end! The "gaude" he brings off with his relics is the best example of his contempt for them—the shoulderblade of a holy Jew's sheep which cures animal diseases, makes livestock multiply, heals a husband's jealousy of his wife; the mitten which increases grain; and the warning that anyone who has done a horrible sin, or any woman who has made her husband a cuckold, will have to stay in their seats. It is droll that the "lewed" people fall for this—whether it illustrates his skill or their ignorance is left ambiguous (though we are told he made parsons his apes as well); but it is such a gross, improbable deception that it puts us on his side and makes us share his pleasure. Everyone who has taught the poem knows the little *frisson* of delight which ripples through a class over this passage, and that sets the tone of one's response throughout. *We* are not of the "lewed" people so easily hoodwinked; thus we become party to his tricks and share his pleasure in them. He was trying for the same effect among the pilgrims—his underlying contempt for them only shows at the end; and the Host is the first to see it, or show he does. . . .

He is impudent. There is something bold-faced and grandly daring in all his discourse and behavior. He is a beardless man with a voice like a goat's, but he is able to hold an audience spellbound. It is abundantly clear that he looks odd—his hair alone, hanging in wax-colored colpons, ought to raise an eyebrow—but he rides *dischevelee,* his hood in his "walet," hair spread on shoulders. He sings aloud—and about love. He claims he was about to wed a wife, and would have a jolly wench in every town. The text he chooses for his sermon is itself a bare-faced bit of braggadocio. Requested by the gentles to tell some moral thing "that we may leere / Some wit," he thinks a moment, downing a draught of ale, upon some "honest thing," then tells them the most honest thing he can think of: he is a fraud and a scoundrel. . . . [H]e can forestall the distaste he provokes by calculated insouciance and flair: he rides *dischevelee,* "all of the newe jet," singing. If you act on top of the world people will believe it, but you must never for a minute show doubt or fear. And he has the actor's genius, is able to sustain the pose; has the verbal skill; has aplomb. It is a choice which requires bravado, intelligence, a quick wit and tongue, and a will. And what nature did not give him in other respects she gave him in these.

Only, it takes its toll.

He is invidious. The force which energizes his charade is an obsessive lust for power in whatever directions he has a capability—say it is libido necessarily redirected or sublimated, but one cannot miss its most basic force, resentment. He is filled with hate. The "avarice" which moves him is not half so much the avarice of getting or having as that of taking away. His will to deprive others, his motive antisocial, sheer, gloating rapacity: the presentation of him could be considered a study of the obsessional or psychopathic character, of the criminal mind. His condescension, which seems amusing directed against the "lewed" people, is only one symptom of his feeling toward all—*all* are ripe to be his gulls. . . . The poorest widow in a village is not beyond his grasp; her children dying of hunger make no impression on him. So at least he says. But he represents himself in this malevolent picture partly out of self-contempt. His enormous hatred includes himself—it is as if he were demanding of the pilgrims that they excuse his villainy or punish it. Why else would anyone admit in public crimes which by rights he would conceal? Hence the abuse the Host unleashes on him is expected, perhaps invited.

—Donald Howard, *The Idea of* The Canterbury Tales (Berkeley: University of California Press, 1976): pp. 349–50, 352–54.

HELEN COOPER ON THE OLD MAN IN THE TALE

[Helen Cooper is Fellow and Tutor of English at University College, Oxford, and author of *Pastoral: Mediaeval into Renaissance* and *The Structure of the Canterbury Tales*.]

What is the old man? His equivalent in the analogues is a wise man or philosopher, even Christ: here he keeps the wisdom, now associated also with old age, and the virtue—a reading of him as evil has to ignore the way Chaucer presents him. He cannot be Death, since death is his greatest desire, and part of the point of the tale, paradoxically, is that death is not a material thing that can be found—the gold is death to the rioters, but only [through] the self-destruction they bring with them. He is not the Wandering Jew, though he has something of the same compelling mythic power. Nor is he *vetus homo,* unredeemed or sinful man, since he knows all about the Redemption, quotes Holy Writ, and sees himself as following 'Goddes wille.' He is what the text says he is: an old man seeking death. The implications of that, however, are extensive.

In the first place, his is a familiar medieval type, though more familiar in visual than literary art. Allegorical pictures of the universality of death invariably show Death leading away the young, the beautiful, the rich, the carefree, and leaving behind cripples, beggars, and the aged, who reach towards him with outstretched hands. The theme had gained extra poignancy at the time of the Black Death, when the plague struck most viciously at the young and healthy—and it is 'pestilence' that is Death's weapon in this story. At one level, the tale is giving verbal form to the pictorial allegory of death. The particular power associated with the old man, however, which has prompted so many attempts to explain him, comes in part at least from his most literal meaning. He is the truth of what the rioters are seeking: life without death. He is not immortal, but like the Wandering Jew or Swift's Struldbrugs, he is cursed with that most terrible of human myths, an infinitely prolonged old age. He has learnt that earthly treasure is valueless compared with a pauper's shroud; the rioters chase off after the gold and find in the gift of Fortune the death they had scorned.

The rioters are 'exemplary' characters: the point of their appearance in a sermon is to warn the congregation off similar vices. They are accordingly never given individual names, and are often referred to by their degrees of sinfulness—'the proudeste', 'the worste'. The figure outside the Tale who most nearly resembles them is however the Pardoner himself. He too is on a quest for treasure, and the quest becomes explicit at the end of the tale, in his double appeal to his congregation and to his pilgrim audience. The Pardoner makes it quite clear why he has come on the pilgrimage: he has only one *entente,* of acquisition, and when he turns to the pilgrims he is aiming to put it into practice. Just as his spurious pardons are a corruption and perversion of penance, so the penitential aim of pilgrimage is corrupted to pecuniary ends. The morality of his tale is similarly perverted for his own unethical purposes.

The rioters find Death at the end of their quest; the Pardoner finds a threat of castration—'Lat kutte hem of!' It is at this point, if anywhere, that the image of the Pardoner as spiritual eunuch is suggested: his Prologue and Tale have insistently deprived things of their potential spiritual meanings, and the Host's threat would show in physical form his lack of spiritual expression. All that happens is that the Pardoner's quest for income is guaranteed unfruitful, and he has to perform his one act of charity and reconciliation in the entire work, in exchanging a kiss with Harry Bailly. The two elder rioters had killed the third 'as in game'; the Knight turns aside the violence that threatens their own 'pleye'. That the Pardoner is so angry, however, adds the final sin of wrath to complete the list: pride, in his contempt for God and his fellow-men; gluttony, in his fondness for wine, and which he himself has associated with the Fall; lechery, in his boasting about wenches, and his other more doubtful sexual practices; envy, in backbiting and defamation; sloth, in his spiritual deadness; and above all, avarice—the sin that was seen as the most threatening of the later Middle Ages by many moralists, including the Parson, who repeats the Pardoner's own text: 'The roote of alle harmes is Coveitise'.

There is one last irony in the tale, in Harry Bailly's outburst,

> 'Thou woldest make me kisse thyn olde breech,
> And swere it were a relyk of a seint,
> Though it were with thy fundament depeint!'

It is the last, and potentially most damaging, reduction of the spiritual to the earthly, for one of the most prized relics of the shrine of St Thomas at Canterbury, to which the pilgrims are making their way, was the saint's filthy breeches, unchanged over the years as part of the process of his mortification of the flesh. A little over a century later another Catholic pilgrim, Erasmus, was appalled by both the unspirituality of the relics and the avarice of their custodians. Chaucer almost certainly knew Langland's valuing of spiritual pilgrimage, the search for truth in the heart, over geographical pilgrimage, and the thought was by no means original with England. Chaucer's Pardoner is a forerunner of the Reformation, not only as

an instance of corruption within the Church and as a peddler of
false pardons, but because he opens the way to questioning the connections between outward forms and spiritual meaning. He
threatens the harmony of this pilgrimage: what he stands for will
destroy the whole basis of pilgrimage, and any possibility of the harmony of a universal church.

—Helen Cooper, *Oxford Guides to Chaucer: The Canterbury Tales.*
(Oxford: Oxford University Press, 1989): pp. 269–71.

HAROLD BLOOM ON THE PARDONER AS THE FIRST NIHILIST

[Harold Bloom is Sterling Professor of the Humanities at
Yale University and Berg Professor of English at New York
University. He is the author of more than twenty books,
including the best-selling *The Western Canon* (1994), and
The Anxiety of Influence (1973), which sets forth Professor
Bloom's theory of the literary relationships between the
great writers and their predecessors.]

It is a critical commonplace to link the Wife of Bath and Falstaff, but
I have seen no speculation on the highly possible descent of Shakespeare's great villains, Iago in *Othello* and Edmund in *King Lear,*
from the Pardoner. Marlowe's hero-villains, Tamburlaine the Great
and even more Barabas, the wily Jew of Malta, clearly made a deep
impression on Shakespeare's portrayal of Aaron the Moor in his first
tragedy, the charnelhouse *Titus Andronicus,* and on that of Richard
III. Between Aaron and Richard on the one hand and Iago and
Edmund on the other, a shadow intervenes, and it seems to belong
to the antithetical Pardoner, who is the outcast of the *Canterbury
Tales.* Even his prologue and tale are outside the apparent structure
of Chaucer's all-but-finished major poem. As a kind of floater, the
Pardoner's Tale is its own world; it resembles nothing else in
Chaucer, yet it seems to me his high point as a poet and in its way
unsurpassable, at one of the limits of art. Donald Howard, musing
on the difference between the Pardoner and his story and the rest of

the Canterbury Tales, compares the Pardoner's intrusion to "the marginal world of medieval aesthetics, the lewd or quotidian drawings in the margins of serious manuscripts," forerunners of Hieronymus Bosch. So pungent are the Pardoner's presence and his narration that the marginal becomes central in Chaucer, inaugurating what Nietzsche was to call "the uncanniest guest," the representation of European nihilism. The link between the Pardoner and Shakespeare's grand negations, Iago and Edmund, seems to me as profound as Dostoevsky's reliance upon Shakespeare's intellectual villains as models for Svidrigailov and Stavrogin.

The Pardoner first appears with his horrible chum, the grotesque Summoner, toward the close of the General Prologue. The Summoner is the equivalent of the thought police who currently afflict Iran; he is a layman who drags supposed spiritual offenders into a religious court. A snooper into sexual relations, he rakes off a percentage of the earnings of all the prostitutes at work in his diocese and blackmails their customers. As narrator of the General Prologue, the Pilgrim Chaucer expresses appreciation for the Summoner's mildness at blackmail: a mere quart of strong red wine each year permits an ongoing sexual relation to continue. Irony for once seems overcome by Chaucer's reluctance to react to the Summoner's moral squalor, which merely helps to provide context for the far more spectacular Pardoner. The Summoner is just an amiable brute, a fit companion for the Pardoner, who plunges us into an inferno of consciousness more Shakespearean than Dantesque because mutable in the highest degree. Chaucer inherits the identity of pardoners and charlatans from the literature and reality of his own times, but the remarkable personality of the Pardoner seems to me his most extraordinary invention.

Pardoners traveled about selling indulgences for sins in defiance of canon law, but rather clearly with church connivance. As lay persons, pardoners were not supposed to preach, but they did, and Chaucer's Pardoner is a superb preacher, surpassing any televangelist currently on the American scene. Critics divide on the Pardoner's sexual nature: is he a eunuch, a homosexual, a hermaphrodite? None of the above, I venture; and in any case Chaucer has seen to it that we just don't know. Perhaps the Pardoner knows; we are not even certain of that. Of the twenty-nine pilgrims, he is much the most questionable, but also much the most intelligent, in that regard almost a rival to Chaucer, the thirtieth pilgrim. The Pardoner's gifts are indeed so formidable that we are compelled to wonder about his long foreground, of which he tells us nothing. A knowing religious hypocrite, trading in spurious relics and daring to traffic in the redemption open through Jesus, he is nevertheless an authentic spiritual consciousness with a powerful religious imagination.

The heart of darkness that is an obscurantist metaphor in Joseph Conrad is all too appropriate a figure for the demoniac Pardoner, who rivals his fictive descendants as a kind of problematic abyss, depraved yet imaginative in the highest degree. One critic of Chaucer, R. A. Shoaf, brilliantly observes of the Pardoner, "He tells himself, his act, every day in his profession; but, to judge from the pattern of his obsession, he knows because he regrets that he cannot buy himself back." What he knows is that his performances, however astonishing, cannot redeem him, and we begin to suspect, as we ponder his spiel and his tale, that something beyond greed and the pride of preaching with power has driven him to his life's work as a professional deceiver. We can never know what it was in Chaucer that could create this first nihilist, at least in literature.

—Harold Bloom, *The Western Canon* (New York: Harcourt Brace & Company, 1994): pp. 119–21.

Works by
Geoffrey Chaucer

The Book of Duchess, 1369–70.

House of Fame, 1372–73.

Parliament of Fowls, 1382.

Troylus and Criseyde, 1382–85.

Legend of Good Women, 1385–86

The Canterbury Tales, 1387–1400.

Works about
Geoffrey Chaucer

Astell, Ann W. *Chaucer and the Universe of Learning*. Ithaca: Cornell University Press, 1996.

Baum, Paul F. *Chaucer: A Critical Appreciation*. Durham, N.C.: Duke University Press, 1958.

Benson, Larry. *Contradictions: from Beowulf to Chaucer*. Brookfield, Vt.: Ashgate Publishing, 1995.

Biscoglio, Frances. *The Wives of the Canterbury Tales and the Tradition of the Valiant Woman of Proverbs 31: 10-31*. San Francisco: Mellen University Press, 1993.

Bloom, Harold. *The Western Canon*. New York: Harcourt Brace & Company, 1994.

———, ed. *Geoffrey Chaucer's the General Prologue to the Canterbury Tales*. New York: Chelsea House Publishers, 1988.

———, ed. *Geoffrey Chaucer's the Knight's Tale*. New York: Chelsea House Publishers, 1988.

Bowden, Muriel. *A Commentary on the General Prologue to the Canterbury Tales*, 2d ed. New York: Macmillan, 1967.

Brewer, D. S., ed. *Chaucer and Chaucerians*. Tuscaloosa: University of Alabama Press, 1966.

Brewer, D. S. *Chaucer*. London: Longmans, 1973.

Bronson, Bertrand H. *In Search of Chaucer*. Toronto: University of Toronto Press, 1960.

Brooks, Harold F. *Chaucer's Pilgrims: The Artistic Order of the Portraits in the Prologue*. London: Methuen, 1962.

Brown, Peter. *Chaucer at Work: The Making of the Canterbury Tales*. London: Longman, 1994.

Calabrese, Michael. *Chaucer's Ovidian Arts of Love*. Gainsville: University Press of Florida, 1994.

Chesterton, G. K. *Chaucer*. London: Faber & Faber.

Coghill, Nevill. *The Poet Chaucer.* London: Oxford University Press, 1967.

Cook, Albert S. "Chaucerian Papers: " *Transactions of the Connecticut Academy of Art and Sciences* 23 (1919): 5–10.

Cunnigham, J. V. "The Literary Form of the Prologue to *The Canterbury Tales.*" *Modern Philology* 49 (1951–52): 172–81.

Dean, James, and Christian Zacher, eds. *The Idea of Medieval Literature: New Essays on Chaucer and Medieval Culture in Honor of Donald R. Howard.* Newark: University of Delaware Press, 1992.

Donaldson, E. Talbot. *Speaking of Chaucer.* Durham, N.C.: Labyrinth, 1983.

————, ed. *Chaucer's Poetry: An Anthology for the Modern Reader.* New York: John Wiley & Sons, 1975.

Fisher, John H. *The Importance of Chaucer.* Carbondale: Southern Illinois University Press, 1992.

Heinrichs, Katherine. *The Myth of Love: Classical Lovers in Medieval Literature.* University Park: Pennsylvania State University Press, 1990.

Hines, John. *The Fabliau in English.* London: Longman, 1993.

Hoffman, Arthur. "Chaucer's Prologue to Pilgrimage: The Two Voices." *ELH* 21 (1954): 1–16.

Howard, Donald, R. "Chaucer the Man." *PMLA* (1949): 823–28.

————. *Chaucer.* New York: E. P. Dutton, 1987.

————. *The Idea of the Canterbury Tales.* Berkeley: University of California Press, 1976.

Jones, Terry. *Chaucer's Knight: The Portrait of a Medieval Mercenary.* London: Methuen, 1994.

Lawlor, John. *Chaucer.* London: Hutchinson University Library, 1968.

Leicester, Marsall. "The Art of Impersonation: A General Prologue to the *Canterbury Tales.*" *PMLA* 95 (1980).

Lumiansky, R. M. *Of Soundry Folk.* Austin: University of Texas Press, 1955.

Mandel, Jerome. *Geoffrey Chaucer: Building the Fragments of the Canterbury Tales*. Rutherford: Fairleigh Dickinson University Press, 1992.

Mann, Jill. *Chaucer and Medieval Estates Satire: The Literature of Social Classes and the General Prologue to the Canterbury Tales*. Cambridge: Cambridge University Press, 1973.

Muscatine, Charles. *Chaucer and the French Tradition*. Berkeley: University of California Press, 1957.

Schoeck, Richard J., and Jerome Taylor, eds. *Chaucer Criticism, Volume I: The Canterbury Tales*. Notre Dame, Ind.: University of Notre Dame Press, 1960.

Speirs, John. *Chaucer the Maker*. Winchester, Mass: Faber & Faber, 1964.

Taylor, Paul. *Chaucer's Chain of Love*. Madison: Fairleigh Dickinson University Press, 1996.

Tuve, Rosamond. "Spring in Chaucer and before Him." *MLN* 52 (1937): 9–16.

Wagenknecht, Edward, ed. *Chaucer: Modern Essays in Criticism*. New York: Oxford University Press, 1959.

Index of
Themes and Ideas

MILLER'S TALE, THE, 49

MONK, 17, 31, 37

NUN, 16

PARDONER: animal imagery and, 31; appearance of, 20; as conde-scending, 98–99; as extraordinary performer, 92, 98–100; as first nihilist, 103–5; as fixed character, 75–76; in *General Prologue,* 19, 20, 37, 75–76, 95–96, 104; greed and, 91, 100, 101–2; as impudent, 99–100; as invid-ious, 100; irony and, 93–94; paradox and, 95–97; as proud, 98, 102; Reformation and, 102–3; Wife of Bath and, 59–60, 75, 86, 96

PARDONER'S PROLOGUE, 91, 93–105; critical views on, 93–105; as dramatic monologue, 93; greed in, 91; paradox and, 95; thematic analysis of, 91

PARDONER'S TALE, 70, 92–105; critical views on, 93–105; as dramatic monologue, 93; greed in, 96–97; irony and, 93–94; old man in, 100–103; paradox and, 95–97; style of, 93–94; thematic analysis of, 92

PARSON, 18–19, 27, 28, 31, 37, 102

PARSON'S PROLOGUE, 33

PLOUGHMAN, 19, 27, 28, 37

PRIORESS, 34–35, 37

REEVE, 19, 25, 37

SCHOLAR, 17

SECOND NUN'S TALE, 86

SERGEANT-AT-LAW, 17, 29, 37

SHIPMAN, 18, 37

SHIPMAN'S TALE, THE, 24, 25, 80, 87

SQUIRE, 16, 27, 37

SUMMONER, 19–20, 25, 30, 37, 104

WIFE OF BATH: antifeminism and, 69, 78–79; appearance of, 18, 71–73; Chaucer's marriage and, 83–87; Falstaff and, 10, 67, 70, 78, 87–90; as fixed character, 75–76; in *General Prologue,* 18, 25, 37, 38, 75–76, 87; husbands of, 60–61, 73, 79, 81–82, 86–88; learnings of, 64–66; marriage and, 25, 59–61, 62–63, 69, 70–71, 76–77, 81–83, 85, 86–88; Pardoner and, 59–60, 75, 86, 96; sensuality of, 18, 66–69, 70; sources of, 74. 78; as symbol of humanity, 79–80; *Tale* of revealing desires of, 80–83; as victorious, 74–77, 79–80; vitality of, 70, 81, 87–90; women satirized by, 69–71